Image, Incarnation,
&
Christian Expansivism

Image, Incarnation, & Christian Expansivism

A Meta-Philosophy of Salvation

MARK S. MCLEOD-HARRISON

 CASCADE *Books* · Eugene, Oregon

IMAGE, INCARNATION, AND CHRISTIAN EXPANSIVISM
A Meta-Philosophy of Salvation

Copyright © 2017 Mark S. McLeod-Harrison. All rights reserved. Except for brief quotations in critical publications or reviews, no part of this book may be reproduced in any manner without prior written permission from the publisher. Write: Permissions, Wipf and Stock Publishers, 199 W. 8th Ave., Suite 3, Eugene, OR 97401.

Cascade Books
An Imprint of Wipf and Stock Publishers
199 W. 8th Ave., Suite 3
Eugene, OR 97401

www.wipfandstock.com

PAPERBACK ISBN: 978-1-5326-0642-7
HARDCOVER ISBN: 978-1-5326-0644-1
EBOOK ISBN: 978-1-5326-0643-4

Cataloguing-in-Publication data:

Names: McLeod-Harrison, Mark S.

Title: Image, incarnation, and Christian expansivism : a meta-philosophy of salvation / Mark S. McLeod-Harrison.

Description: Eugene, OR: Cascade Books 2017 | Includes bibliographical references and index.

Identifiers: ISBN 978-1-5326-0642-7 (paperback) | ISBN 978-1-5326-0644-1 (hardcover) | ISBN 978-1-5326-0643-4 (ebook)

Subjects: LCSH: Salvation outside the church | Christianity and other religions | Evangelistic work—philosophy | Theology of religions (Christian theology) | Salvation—Christianity

Classification: BT759 M243 2017 (paperback) | BT579 (ebook)

Manufactured in the U.S.A.   03/24/17

Unless otherwise noted, Scripture quotations are from the New Revised Standard Version Bible, copyright © 1989 National Council of the Churches of Christ in the United States of America. Used by permission. All rights reserved.

For Phil Smith,
who eighteen years ago saw fit
to hire me as his colleague
and then became my friend.

And in memory of
Karen Bates Smith
psychologist, composer, photographer,
friend.

Contents

Preface | ix
Acknowledgements | xxi

Chapter 1
Setting the Salvific Stage | 1

Chapter 2
On Being the Literal Image of God | 20

Chapter 3
Existentially Problematic Salvific Exclusivism | 45

Chapter 4
Why We Should Preach the Gospel | 58

Chapter 5
Toward an Expansive Gospel | 81

Chapter 6
On Becoming Second Incarnations | 106

Appendix
Theistic Irrealism's Ancestors | 125

Bibliography | 149
Index | 151

Preface

> There is salvation in no one else, for there is no other name under heaven given among mortals by which we must be saved. (Acts 4:12)

> Jesus said to him, "I am the way, and the truth, and the life. No one comes to the Father except through me." (John 14: 6)

Christianity is, in some sense, exclusivistic in its claims. The question is, what sense should we give to that sense? I attempt to clarify particular understandings of exclusivism and propose an alternative exclusivism for both. The first sense is what can be called "access exclusivism," and it is the immediate circumstance for my writing. This sort of exclusivism says that *our* way is the *only* way to gain access to the salvific work of Christ. Of course, *our* way depends on the speaker. In my experience, many people—and here I have in mind Protestant Christians with very conservative or even fundamentalist leanings—think that their way of appropriating the gospel is the only way. One easy means to illustrate is to point to the many conservative Protestants who remain suspicious of Roman Catholics and are inclined to evangelize them. Even after four years of taking Bible, theology, and church history courses at the evangelical Christian university where I teach, students often still refer to Roman Catholicism as "that religion." I'm astonished every time.

The second sort of exclusivism is ontological. It seems to me that the verses quoted above should be understood in this way, viz., the work of Christ in his incarnation, life, death, and resurrection provide the necessary and sufficient grounds for the salvation of humanity. I quibble with this claim. However, I do think that a certain narrow-mindedness often attaches to it so that we end up thinking (and otherwise acting) as if our understanding of the ontology of Christ is the only legitimate way to think of it. I reject that view as well.

But this is not merely a book of criticism. In point of fact, my concern is fundamentally pastoral, even though the essay is a philosophical one. I propose a sort of inclusivism about the work of Christ that I call "expansivism." Expansivism holds to an exclusive claim about the necessity and sufficiency of the work of Christ but is ontologically pluralistic about that work. In short, expansivism holds that there are many true but logically conflicting ways in which the work of Christ is understood. So while the incarnation, life, death, and resurrection of Christ are central, what actually happened in that work is describable in conflicting yet true ways. Expansivism is rooted in a larger account of the world's many ontologies I call "theistic irrealism." I've developed that view in detail elsewhere but say enough about it below to show how it works when applied to Christian salvation.[1]

Given my experience both in the church and in the Christian colleges where I've taught, I thought finding a scholarly audience would be easy. After all, the view I had in mind to explore and critique seemed fairly commonplace in the evangelical church—some of my students providing good examples of it. But apparently how scholars think is substantially different from how some other Christians think. Many of my students have something very specific in mind when they talk about being "saved" and they provide good examples of the access exclusivism that is part of my concern. Some scholars, on the other hand and as I'll illustrate below, think we can ignore this sort of exclusivism and thereby it will disappear. Nevertheless, there is a scholarly impetus to my writing, found in two sources. First, there are some brief comments of Philip Quinn and Kevin Meeker in the introduction to their book *The Philosophical Challenge of Religious Diversity* where they encourage further thought on the nature of an inclusive approach to understanding the diversity of religions. Second, there is William Lane Craig's essay "No Other Name" and his work in evangelism over a good deal of his life. Bill was my M.A. thesis supervisor and for a brief time a colleague at Westmont College. His work in philosophy is widely known but I've found the least convincing part of his output the essay noted above. I wanted to write a response to Bill's essay.

---

1. McLeod-Harrison, *Make/Believing*.

Preface

When I began to write about the critical material, I thought th[ey] were fairly clear, the options describable, and the solutions more [or less] standardly codified. Of course, there are a variety of views about th[e nature] of faith and how one should practice it. But are there really disagre[ements] about how one must access the work of Christ? Don't we all rely o[n faith?] In some sense, yes, we all rely on faith. Yet I believe there are disagre[ements] and that they are not merely philosophical or theological but [also] sociological, and psychological. To illustrate this claim, consider [my] few forays into writing a philosophical reflection on the subject of exclusivity.

Those forays were met with some interesting responses. I [sent an] ancestor of chapter 4 to a well-known journal in philosophy of r[eligion,] albeit a "secular" journal and not one rooted in any particular "take" [on] philosophy of religion or philosophical theology. It is a journal i[n which] I've published before. Here is the blind-reviewer's reply:

> My recommendation is to reject this paper. It is well-written, an[d] the logic of the arguments seems to me right on target. Howeve[r,] the topic is so far beyond the pale of what I consider articles i[n] [this journal] should be about that I cannot recommend the pa[]per's publication. Indeed, while reading this article I felt I ha[d] been transported to some other realm where people worry abou[t] witches, poison apples, spells, etc. Inside such a world-view, on[e] can, of course, construct all sorts of philosophical issues and writ[e] tantalizing papers proposing and criticizing solutions for them[.] But why enter such an absurd world-view in the first place?[2]

When I read this response to one of my evangelical colleagues, I [won]dered aloud at what should count as philosophy of religion if one ca[n't care] about issues that concern huge swaths of the church.

Perhaps even more surprising, however, was the response [of] evangelical scholars who seemed to be having an equally hard tim[e see]ing (but for different reasons) that anyone in the church actually h[olds the] sort of view which I describe in chapter 1 as Christian salvific excl[usivism] and which I critically engage in chapter 3. This is illustrated by a [certain] journal's response to my work, this time an evangelically rooted p[hiloso]phy of religion journal. They seemed overly cautious, it seems to m[e, about] publishing an ancestor of some of the work I do in chapters 2 and [3. In] part of the problem was mine, as I was admittedly having a diffic[ult]

---

2 From an email reply from the journal rejecting the paper.

xi

formulating the position of the Christian salvific exclusivist. But not all was my problem. One of the reviewers for that journal seem puzzled with the idea that anyone—even the evangelicals with whom he works daily—would actually hold the narrow exclusivism I was rejecting. Of course, the folks with whom this reviewer works are scholars. It is the other folks in the church that I want to give due.

I too sometimes wonder about the worldview in which traditional Christianity is embedded and the comparison to poisoned apples and spells can sometimes be apt. Yet with my colleague, I believe the reviewer for the "secular" journal missed the point, and that, it seems to me, is rather sad. Or perhaps it is just narrow-minded. My goal is to encourage more open-mindedness about how Christians think about salvation *from within the faith*. The reviewer apparently failed to see some very important features of the *de facto* Christian landscape and therefore merely wrote off the exclusivistic view I'm engaging. Indeed, the reviewer seemed to write off those who even think that way. In my experience, many people do hold salvific exclusivism, sometimes quite strong versions of it. Unfortunately, some scholars would rather not see, or at least would rather not deal with, the views of everyday Christians as opposed to mere armchair theorizing about the Christian faith or religion more generally.

In addition to the review from the evangelically rooted journal, others of my scholarly evangelical friends simply think better of the evangelical church, suggesting that exclusivism is not really the "official" view of the church and therefore we should more or less ignore it. These folks, however, seem to have taken up a similar mindset to the evangelical reviewer, not toward pluralism, but toward inclusivism. They think that no one worth paying attention to in the church would hold the more radical sort of exclusivism I want to discuss. So the reviewer of the "secular" journal didn't think very highly of people for whom the exclusivism issue might in fact be an issue and the evangelical scholars think perhaps too highly of their own enlightened understanding of our access to salvation, thinking that pretty much everyone in the church would agree with them. If these responses are not rooted in cultural, sociological, and psychological reasons, I wonder what does root them?

In some sense, I did not find the rather dismissive attitude of the above-quoted reviewer from the "secular" journal surprising. A set of extreme positions exists on both ends of the spectrum, one quite exclusivistic and the other quite pluralistic. The reviewer's finding my discussion reminiscent of poison apples and spells is the sort of thing one sometimes hears from the extremely pluralistic end of the salvific spectrum. Religion, if it points to an afterlife at all, points to a vague or unspecific one. All paths lead to salvation, if that is even the right term—on such views the very notion of salvation may be suspect. More often than not, if such views have a notion of salvation, they are not other-world oriented at all (as more traditional views often are). Instead they take religion to be a cultural or societal creation that is supposed to help us get on in this life. On the other end of the salvific spectrum one can find an other-worldliness that barely pays attention to how we live here and now. There the path to that salvation is indeed very narrow and those of other faiths are not on the path and sometimes thought of as not even looking for it. Of course, there are many views in between and an excellent case can be made from the Scripture that salvation is neither just about the future afterlife nor just about the present life but about both.

In spite of such responses, I've written the book. Here are my reasons. First, both reviewers and the evangelical scholars I've talked to about this seem to me to get it wrong; *lots* of people in fact hold Christian salvific exclusivism, sometimes quite radical versions of it. Second, such folks often make up huge swaths of some churches, and I care about the church. Third, in addition to philosophical concerns, I have pastoral concerns. It seems to me that philosophers too often concern themselves only with *theoria* and not much with *praxis*. This book concerns itself with both, at least so far as philosophy can take one in a pastoral direction.

My main concern in the book is this question: How do humans access the work that Christ has done and how might that affect our understanding of the incarnation? I do not argue for the claim that Christ is, in fact, the only path to God nor do I take up religious pluralism or argue against it, at least in any detail. I attempt to provide two things: first, a clear account and fair-minded critique of Christian salvific exclusivism, and second, a cogent alternative to exclusivism. In doing so, I hope the work takes Scripture seriously. I also hope it captures our experience of ourselves as humans in a way that places each of us uniquely and individually in history. This is an "in-house" project, written for traditional Christians by a Christian philosopher. Yet it is also meant to show how Christianity could be the truth about salvation while opening the possibility that many people from all religious walks are on the path to salvation. Thus, it is both conservative and quite open.

Preface

What follows tries to take the typical *traditional* Christian believer's point of view seriously while providing an alternative to it that sustains all that is good about the tradition and yet opens the door to a more liberating sense of God's love and grace. Of course, there are many Christians who do not hold traditional views of the faith. These folks can often be described as revisionist Christians. While the Christian faith does sometimes need to be revised, where revision is needed and where it is not is not a bright and clear line. Since I view myself as a serious Christian who believes what is taught in the traditional creeds—God created the world; Jesus is God incarnate and lived, died, and was resurrected; the Holy Spirit lives within us and is calling us into a salvific relationship with God—I'm concerned to remain within the bounds of orthodoxy. But at the same time, I don't believe in poisoned apples either. The traditional Christian faith, for all its foibles, is not overcome or shown false by comparing it unfavorably to fairy tales.

So I attempt below to think through the more traditional views of my sisters and brothers on how one can enter the kingdom of heaven. I suggest a middle-of-the-road position that doesn't take us all the way from salvific exclusivity to religious salvific plurality, from a single-path, single-access Christian evangelistic stance to an all-religions-are-equally-good path. To remain an orthodox Christian one must affirm the uniqueness of the gospel message of the Scriptures and tradition. But affirming that message does not entail affirming the narrow interpretation of how that message is engaged by humans in various and sundry historical circumstances. In the end, however, the view I propose will probably not make the reviewer from the "secular" journal I quoted above happy or the very conservative evangelical Christian stand up to dance. It is, however, meant to help both sides see that there is a good way to remain thoroughly Christian and yet consistently open about the gospel's reach. So what follows is not just a theoretical study. It is meant to be helpful for those of us in the church who care about how to live our lives in faithfulness to God, the Scriptures, and the tradition.

To contextualize my claims, permit a few general words about the tenor of what follows. God scraped together some dirt, breathed into it, and humans became living beings. Dirt plus the breath of God makes humans living beings. There's no mention of bodies as separate from our minds, emotions, wills, or souls. Humans are, from the beginning, inseparably rooted in the dirt. From dust we are made and to dust we will return. But we will not stay merely dust, for we are holy humus, dirt made fertile by

God's creative spirit. Salvation is no disembodied notion; it's not merely of the soul. We are resurrected bodily into new life with all our spiritual richness. As spiritualized bodies in space and time, we are forever historical creatures. That broad-stroke picture is behind this entire essay.

Christian philosophy should be holistic, speaking not merely to the mind, but to the heart; not merely to the soul, but to the embodied and historical beings God made us to be. This is a pastoral way to think of ourselves. While not all philosophy needs to be pastoral (philosophy of mathematics, for example, probably need not be concerned about people's souls), pastoral philosophy is one branch of Christian thought, a branch seeking to bring theoretical concerns together with spiritual issues. As such, it engages the Christian tradition as a means to help people resolve theoretical issues where they overlap with the existential. Let me illustrate briefly. My book *Repairing Eden: Humility, Mysticism and the Existential Problem of Religious Diversity* takes a pastoral philosophy approach to the challenge of how Christians can find their faith drifting away when exposed to the diversity of religions. While rationally there may be no issue with Christianity being true or rationally accepted in the face of religious diversity, once one is exposed to the many ways of being religious, some folk find themselves just no longer able to believe in the Christian way. After providing philosophical and theological analyses of the existential situation, I propose and explain that such people can (and should) seek humility and, indeed, a mystical experience with Christ as a solution to the lived circumstances in which they find themselves.

So in the present essay I turn the aims of pastoral philosophy to the notion of Christian salvation. But since my first forays into pastoral philosophy came into print, a new movement has gained steam in philosophical-theology circles, viz., analytic theology. I've found that the tools of analytic philosophy and theology can help introduce and consider pastoral concerns, contrary to what one of the founders of analytic theology suggests.[3] I wish to identify at least part of this work as analytic theology. The approach I take follows the sort of tack within analytic theology suggested by William Abraham, where essentially contested concepts are taken up, parables found useful, and Basil Mitchell is something close to the patron saint.[4] Analytic theology takes the tools of analytic philosophy and applies

---

3. See Rea "Introduction," 18. Rea claims there that the point of analytic theology is not to make us wise, but to build models and clarify theology concepts.

4. Abraham, "Turning Theological Water into Wine," 1–16.

them to theological issues. Analytic theology is fairly nascent and perhaps as it matures it will overcome some its potential risks. One of those risks is that it can drift too far from its revelatory scriptural constraints, casting about the heavens for conceptual tools the scriptural authors would never have considered. This essay attempts to avoid that problem by reflecting on various scriptural passages relevant to its topic. However, I'm not doing exegesis as biblical scholars might but rather philosophical work that hopes to illumine those passages. Nevertheless, it does sometimes cast about the heavens, but only in an effort to explain the Scripture.

Another risk of analytic theology is to remove theology from its appropriate home in the life of prayer. Theology, be it analytic or some other sort, ought to always lead one to one's knees in worship before the Lord of the universe. The subject of salvation should perhaps especially encourage one to worship, as worship should be the result of true salvation. Once we are fully present to God I believe we will continue doing philosophy. However, then we will understand it more clearly as an aspect of our prayer to God. So my intent is to write an essay that is pastoral analytic philosophical theology. Chapters 2, 3, and in particular have that flavor, but the entire message tries to reflect on the truly creative nature God provides to us as well as our individual response, in our particular historical circumstances, to the loving gospel of Jesus Christ.

Little is more existential for the Christian believer than salvation. By "existential" I do not intend to pick out a complex idea but simply mean how we actually live our lives. One branch of existential philosophy, by that definition, is pastoral philosophy. One point of this essay is to extend the sorts of things one can do with a pastoral philosophical approach. Paul Moser explores the notion of "cruciform wisdom" which, he proposes, ought to be the pinnacle of the practice of Christian philosophy.[5] While I believe there are some issues with the approach he takes,[6] I think that if one is to take something akin to Moser's approach, one should emphasize that the life of the Spirit cannot be, in the end, separated from the life of the mind. "The wind blows where it chooses, and you hear the sound of it, but you do not know where it comes from or where it goes. So it is with everyone who is born of the Spirit" (John 3:8). As such, this essay, although philosophical, overlaps with questions of spiritual formation. I don't believe ultimately

---

5. See, for example, Moser, *Jesus and Philosophy* and Moser and McFall, "Introduction."

6. Kenyon and McLeod-Harrison "Love, Wisdom and (Christian) Philosophy," and "The Veneration of Truth: How Analytic Theorizing Can Make Us Wise," 6.

that the notions of theological justification can or should be separated from sanctification. Whether the essay approaches cruciform wisdom can be left to the reader to decide. I believe, however, that good spiritual formation is never far from telling us the truth about ourselves and our beliefs. That truth, if this essay is generally right, is much richer and more diverse than many accounts of (exclusivistic) salvation indicate.

That brings me to what sorts of things can be done with pastoral philosophy. One is to point out and bring clarity to existential problems with the Christian faith, which this essay attempts to do in some parts. A second function is to help us look not just at abstract accounts of philosophical notions but to consider how such notions actually work in people's lives. While this essay does not approach the sort of detail one might desire on that latter point, I hope it opens the door to the details. That is, this work attempts to provide a broad sense of the uniqueness that we individual humans bring to God in our need for salvation. In this, I trust it both reflects real people and the witness of the Scriptures. Jesus did not, in fact, treat the people he met in a cookie-cutter fashion. He treated them as the unique individuals they were. That is what we all long for, isn't it; to be treated, accepted, and loved for the unique people we are? This book is intended to help us begin to think about not only how God engages us, but how we engage God in the process of sanctification, which, in the end, cannot be separated from justification. We come into the presence of God after being made holy and that takes not just the work of Christ but the work of our entire beings: body, soul, heart, and mind.

What are my pastoral concerns? A sort of unease bubbles up about exclusivism in various contexts. Inside the church's kitchen, there are two pots boiling. First, there can be a potential existential crisis for those on the extremely conservative or more fundamentalist end of the church. Some of us have been taught or come to believe in a very narrow understanding of the ways in which we humans may access the gift of God's salvation. What happens, then, when two people have conflicting accounts of that access? This sort of existential problem can lead to a real crisis of faith for individual believers, a crisis that sometimes leads folk to leave the faith altogether.

The second issue internal to the church is the unhappy way in which we treat conflicting notions of salvation. Unfortunately, this issue can be generalized to disagreements over any theological reality—salvation, atonement, God's place relative to time, the nature of God's providence, etc. These internal conflicts can be very damaging and while it is all well and good to suggest that we Christians should "live and let live," we often don't, won't, or can't. Historically we have burned a good many people over theological disagreement; we continue to fire theological faculty and oust beloved pastors or other members from our fellowships.[7] Even the churches most epistemically generous can still, at the end of the day, be suspicious of those with whom they theologically disagree. The road to hell is paved with good intentions, but bad theology is bad theology. So think those with the power and matches. If there were a way to see, as committed, Christ-followers that those among us with whom we disagree do not actually have false beliefs or accounts, but have perfectly viable alternative positions *that are equally true* as are our own, we could not merely tolerate but actually embrace our sisters and brothers with delight. This boiling pot has been on the church kitchen's back burner a long time, but the flame can flare up anytime. It is not always clear when someone crosses the line into heresy, but at least there should be a clear recognition that many conflicting positions within the church are orthodox. An ontological approach to this matter could be more peace-making than a merely epistemological tack.

Outside the church, the concerns are of a different order. Often the gospel is presented to those around us as being a "singular way." Indeed, evangelical Christians themselves often worry about the breadth of the gospel: can those who have never heard the gospel be saved? Pluralist approaches are not, in the end, open to evangelicals or theologically conservative Christians of any stripe. While there are many mansions in the Father's house, the foundation that supports them all is the actual, historical work of Jesus. A more lively option for evangelicals is inclusivism. Inclusivistic accounts of the gospel allow those who "follow the light" to be saved. Scripture allows as much when it includes the ancient Hebrews, who had never heard of Christ, to be saved and indicates as well that everyone has some light to follow should they choose to. But what is the appropriate shape to inclusivism? Is it merely an inclusivism of access or does it reach deeper into ontology? Inclusivism as an approach to salvation has not received the sort of attention that it might have.

The overall goal of this book is to add something to the inclusivism discussion. I want to press beyond the questions of access and reach all the way to the ontology of the work of Christ. How should we understand the work of Christ as the only way (ontologically) to come to God through the power of the Holy Spirit while allowing that some (and perhaps many) who

---

7. See, for some examples, Madueme, "Adam and Eve: An Evangelical Impasse?" 165.

do not know about Jesus directly can be saved? I want to suggest that the work of Christ, while rooted in the biblical accounts, can be understood in a variety of ways. But this is no mere epistemological point; I will present a way of thinking about the ontology of the work of Christ as fixed on one level but plural on another level. So I will not be doing exegetical work or even, in the traditional sense, theological work. Instead I'll be doing philosophical work, developing a philosophy of salvation.

Behind my concern with inclusivism, however, is not merely the worry that those who don't hear the gospel can't be saved, but also a feature of humans that can be (and perhaps often is) overlooked in Christian theology. In our emphasis on the image of God as something all humans share, as well as in our emphasis on the fact that all humans sin, we sometimes pass over in silence the fact that each human is unique. But the uniqueness of each human person, both in circumstance and perhaps also in nature, is something that understandings of salvation don't typically find important.

Salvation, then, is a doctrine of the Christian faith rich in nuance and complexity. This essay, however, is a limited-scope, meta-study of salvation. Yet I want to emphasize that I take this to be a work consonant with evangelical theology and philosophy. In that regard, while the book argues for an inclusivist notion of human access to Christ's salvation, it remains exclusivist about the fact that in Christ and Christ alone does one find the ontological basis of salvation. In that sense, at least, it remains firmly exclusivist and firmly within the evangelical camp. But it does not rest with a narrow notion of human access. It instead takes the human access question to suggest that we need a broader understanding of the ontology of salvation—the nature of the work of Christ. On that topic the book holds that Christ and his work remain absolutely central—ontologically necessary and sufficient—to salvation. Yet it is wide enough that any number of ontological accounts consistent with the core account are not only viable and *possibly* true, but viable and *actually* true, even though competing with each other.

Chapter 1 describes various options in the field dealing with access to the gospel. Chapter 2 turns to a (analytic) theological justification of the notion that the image of God in us is not merely a universal image shared by all, but also a *unique* image, special to each of us. Chapter 3 takes up the existential challenge to a too-narrow notion of access to salvation noted above, while chapter 4 broadens the approach to a modest inclusivism, the result of which is to shift our thinking about why the gospel should be preached. Chapter 5 approaches the broader issue of the ontology of salvation by presenting some core philosophical ideas about how to approach questions surrounding ontological pluralism and a more direct application of those ideas to the issue of Christian salvation. Chapter 6 returns to the theological theme of chapter 3 by taking up the issue of how salvation works out as we live our lives. It turns, in short, from justification to sanctification and explains how the approach laid out in the rest of the book might influence our understanding of ourselves as those developing in our salvation.

Underlying all of this is a concern for pastoral care, both for those inside and outside the church. So while my intended audience is the evangelical church in all its various but biblically committed stripes, the path to reaching my goal takes some curvy turns. Hence, my concerns are multiple. Because the book does not take a straight line from beginning to end, others, besides evangelicals, might learn from the essay.

Acknowledgements

When I read books, I always pay attention to the acknowledgements since I know how important people are in the life of a writer and, indeed, in the lives of us all. So here are mine.

First, I want people to know the value of having my son, Micah, buzzing around the room making train and car noises, dragging me away from writing to take him to Whistle Stop (the best model-train store in Portland, Oregon) or the Portland Zoo or Al's Garden Center. That's what was going on when I started this book. Nowadays, he is still buzzing around the room, but talking about his latest idea for his own book themed around some very sophisticated animals and reading science fiction and following it up with books about physics. Micah is on the (autism) spectrum and finds it difficult to deal with death, dying, illness, and generally any kind of loss (including his books, camera, or other personal items). In short, he sometimes is challenged by the "catastrophes" of everyday life. For him, not being able to find a friend or family member in a crowd draws out what can only be described as a death-moan.

So a gospel that includes a dying person hanging on a cross, even where that person is God and will come back alive in a couple of days, is deeply disturbing to him. Micah's concrete understanding of the nature of death has not yet been overcome by what I hope someday will be an equally concrete sense of resurrection. I've learned, from Micah, just how disturbing Jesus' death actually is. But the Jesus who hung on that cross will not leave my son out of the kingdom because he can't accept such a death. Just the opposite. When the all-knowing and apparently quite frustrated male disciples tried to keep the children at bay from Jesus and the importance of

Acknowledgements

their "adult" business, Jesus turned the situation on its head. Setting a child in their midst, Jesus said that unless a person becomes like a child, he will not see the kingdom of heaven.

Micah has been set in the midst of my life and work. His rejection of the standard gospel line reminds me daily of the openness of God's love for each of us in our uniqueness. And when he buzzes by me while I'm trying to write, I have to remember that what seems to be important business to me is not always the business of the kingdom. In short, Jesus shows up to tell me that I need to be as a child to enter the kingdom with my son. I thank Micah for helping me keep my priorities straight, at least some times.

I also thank my wife, Susan, for sharing her many thoughtful insights with me; how Jesus interacts with children as spiritual giants among us is her observation, not mine. She, as always, is the person who keeps me grounded. She too is a writer and blogger who imparts wonderful insights into the nature of God (see http://www.mothergodexperiment.com/). And then there is Salem, who at two-and-a-half always wants to "do a project" with me and who takes me away from writing, but almost always makes me laugh.

I want to thank George Fox University for a sabbatical during the fall term of 2013 in which ancestors of several chapters of this book were written. I also want to thank all the journal reviewers who rejected or otherwise commented on ancestors of various parts of this book. Your comments made me work harder to clarify what I wanted to say but also made me realize how far from the concrete facts of the church philosophers can sometimes get. It is easy for us scholars to forget what some folks in the church are like. But we ignore them at the peril of the church and, I think, the kingdom of God. Some material appeared in other places in somewhat different form. For permission to reprint the published material I thank *Philosophia Christi* (Vol 16, No. 1 2013) in which "Christianity's Many Ways of Salvation" appeared. More information about *Philosophia Christi* can be found at www.epsociety.org. I also thank *The Journal of Analytic Theology* (Vol 2, 2014, 140–59) in which appeared "On Being the Literal Image of God: Rethinking Human Essence as Uniqueness."

Finally, this book is dedicated to two very fine friends Phil Smith is my friend, colleague, and chair of my department. He is one of the finest Christians I know. He's also a good, rooted philosopher. When he reads papers I've written, he often summarizes what I'm trying to say better than I say it. The great thing is, I can then use his phrasing to communicate

Acknowledgements

more clearly than I can on my own! But he is also one of the wisest people I know. He is a wonderful colleague and chair and has become one of my very good friends. The other person I'll have to thank in memoriam. Karen Bates Smith, Phil's spouse of many years, was a person who saw the truth and pursued it in the context of her day to day life. I first met Karen over dinner with Phil as I interviewed for the position I now hold. I was an Episcopalian hoping to join a Quaker department of religious studies. When I found Karen had, at the time, recently converted to Catholicism, I felt a sense of relief. I knew I would be welcomed into this Quaker community. Karen was a therapist, musician, composer, and photographer. She excelled at each. Her loss to Phil and their larger family is deeply felt. She now lives and moves and has her being more fully and deeply. May light perpetual shine on her.

── Chapter 1 ──

Setting the Salvific Stage

God's expansive salvation is the lead actor in this essay, with the image of God and the incarnation as supporting cast. My originating intuition is that the oft-times narrowly construed understanding of salvation some Christians hold does neither the Scriptures nor human individuality nor the love of God justice. That is the starting place. But although the nature of salvation and our human access to it are my main themes, the background topics of image and incarnation are important for it is from them that my claims about salvation and human access flow. Without some grasp of the theological notions of the image of God, which all humans—including Jesus—share, it is difficult to understand what need there is for an incarnation and, by extension, what need there is for the salvation that the incarnation and the death and resurrection of Jesus provides.

This chapter introduces some central terms and notions to which I appeal through the book. Section I presents what I call "Christian salvific exclusivism." Section II considers Christian salvific pluralism and Christian salvific inclusivism.

I

In order to set the context for the ensuing discussion, let's begin with a brief description of what I call "Christian salvific exclusivism." Christian salvific exclusivism (CSE) includes three components. I call them the metaphysical realist, the ontological monistic, and the access components. First, the metaphysical realist component.

1. There is only one true description of reality, including salvific reality. The Christian description of salvific reality is that one true description.[1]

This component is typically rooted in an overall commitment to metaphysical realism where (for the most part) reality is what it is independent of human noetic contributions to the nature of that reality. William Alston notes that most religious believers are realists about their religious beliefs.[2] The metaphysical-realist component of CSE tries to capture that commitment. It is natural for Christians to think of reality as largely (human) mind-independent because, after all, *God*, not humans, created the world. Thus, it is no surprise that the Christian salvific exclusivist has a commitment to metaphysical realism somewhere as a backdrop for her thinking about the world and God's role in it. If she did not, it would be hard to see, initially at any rate, how her claims to exclusivism would be founded. Exceptions can, of course, be made to a global metaphysical realism. For example, when I am thinking, that fact alone makes it so that I'm thinking, and so sometimes reality directly depends on one's mind. Also sometimes we construct parts of reality, for example, marriage and legal entities such as corporations. For the holder of CSE, such exceptions do not extend to the religious realm; religion is not merely a detached language game with no root in independent facts. Just the reverse. Christian claims to reality, where true, are the basis for the rest of the facts about the world.

Now to the ontological monist component.

2. The one true description of the Christian faith tells us that entering into a proper relationship with God through Jesus Christ in the power of the Holy Spirit is necessary and sufficient to be saved. Christ's incarnate work on earth—birth, death, resurrection—provide the monistic ontological basis for salvation.

---

1. In fact, those who hold to a metaphysically realist position about salvation are likely to hold a metaphysically realist position about vast stretches of the rest of reality as well. This may rest on their beliefs that God created the world and that it is objectively independent of human thinkers. There are, of course, exceptions to this suggestion, but we needn't enter that discussion here.

2. See Alston, "Realism."

Setting the Salvific Stage

The monistic ontology of salvation is entailed by 1. Accepting 1 commits CSE to a (general) monistic ontology whereby I mean that there is only one way the world is. That ontologically monistic understanding extends to the conditions described by Scripture and made true by Jesus and his work. The nature of that work can ultimately be described (truly) in only one way.

Finally consider the access component.

3. A particular and unique necessary and sufficient human means grants access to the proper salvific relationship to God through Jesus Christ.

It is important to note that in one sense Jesus is the access to salvation, a point meant to be captured by 2. God calls humans into a salvific relationship through the work of Christ in the power of the Holy Spirit. As such, we could say Jesus is the path to salvation in God. "I am the way, the truth, and the life," says Jesus, "no one comes to the Father but through me." The particular or unique *human means* of accessing that path, as opposed to the path itself, is the focus of this third component. This access is necessary and sufficient (on the human side) for entering into the salvific relationship with Jesus Christ.

One who holds all three components is a Christian salvific exclusivist. Not only is there a singular true description of the (larger) created and uncreated order (the created world and the divine world, one might say) but that description includes both a description of the ontological basis for salvation (Christ's work) and a description of the means of accessing Christ. It is this sort of account of the Christian order of things that has motivated, at least in part, much that has gone on in the name of Christian evangelism and missionary activity. If, in order to be saved, one must access the gospel of Jesus Christ through a particular human means (let's say conscious faith in the work of Jesus), then people need to hear of the gospel of Jesus. Hence, Christians preach and engage in other evangelistic missionary work. I am opposed to neither, but I believe the basis on which we engage in such activities needs to be different from what we often believe (based on CSE, at least).

The phrase "particular and unique means" from 3 stands in need of analysis. The most natural reading is that there is a single and fairly simple means of access. Perhaps the most frequent (Protestant) account would be that one is saved by "faith alone." But the term "faith" needs analysis too. It is an understatement to say that Scripture itself is not completely clear on this topic. Consider the contrast between the Pauline corpus with its emphasis on faith alone and the Jamesian "faith without works is dead." No less a theologian than Martin Luther worried that the book of James, along with Hebrews and John's Revelation, didn't belong in the canon because they conflicted with Paul. James was, in Luther's often-quoted phrase, "an epistle of straw."

What is faith? It is certainly true that in many New Testament contexts where salvation is considered, faith is part of the discussion or at least in the background. Yet it is not always explicit. Jesus himself gives different salvific directions to his interlocutors. Consider Jesus' response to the rich young man's question, what must I do to be saved? Jesus is direct. After a brief discussion of whether the young man has followed the law (he has!), Jesus tells him to go, sell everything he owns, give it to the poor, and come follow Jesus. (A very high bar to reach, it might be added, especially for us relatively wealthy Western Christians.) No explicit mention is made of believing that Jesus is the Messiah. Although one might argue that faith would be involved in such a move by the rich young man, one wonders if hope would be enough. Or perhaps not even hope. Perhaps the young man, having followed, apparently, the law rigorously from his youth, was a particularly strong A-type personality, one who naturally fell in with following the rules strictly. Perhaps he believed, hence, not in Jesus' grace but instead sought to follow Jesus in the way in which he had always sought to follow the law. Perhaps he believed that following Jesus was the means of accessing salvation but did not have faith or trust in Jesus. Or suppose the circumstances were different again. What if the young man just followed Jesus because his parents taught him to, as many young people might even today? Such a person might participate in all the right things (follow the law!) but not really believe in Christ and certainly not trust Christ for his salvation. It's just a community thing one does.

Now consider Jesus' response to the woman at the well. He engages her in a theological discussion about worship at the end of which she is convinced that Jesus is the Messiah. (Or almost—she still is wondering "can this be the Christ?") She becomes the first evangelist for Jesus being "the savior of the world" as her Samaritan neighbors later state it. This Samaritan woman is not asked to sell what she has. Jesus doesn't even ask her to follow him. He simply reveals (to someone not a Jew) that true worship is worship in spirit and truth and that translated into knowing who the Messiah is. Note, too, that in neither the case of the rich young man nor the Samaritan woman does Jesus' interlocutor have any sense that Jesus will die on the cross within a few short months, let alone that he will be raised from the dead.

Of course, in both cases one can read the passages as ones in which Jesus is calling for faith in himself. "Come follow me" demands, perhaps, as much. But the term "faith" is too broad and loose a term. I want to point toward what I will call the "interior framework" of faith, for interior frameworks of faith will be distinct from one another. Faith is, I suggest, different for each of us or, at least, for many of us. What the rich young man experiences as the call to faith demands his giving up his wealth. In the story about the woman at the well, Jesus treats her with respect and dignity, engages her theological questions, and, so to speak, "sees into her soul" in a way no one else ever had. Her response to faith doesn't require her to give up her wealth but to respond to the healing—emotional, intellectual, and spiritual—that Jesus provides. Her excited response "Come, see a man who told me all that I ever did. Can this be the Christ?" indicates how important Jesus' acceptance of her as a complete person was.

To get at what I mean by "interior framework" we have to begin with the basic notion of faith. To have faith might be thought of as a certain set of propositional attitudes—belief or acceptance of a proposition—and/or an attitude of trust toward a person—say God. But what surrounds that faith or the steps by which one fulfills the obligations of faith may be quite different for different people. Some might think faith calls them to attend church, others to feed the poor, still others to deal with their failing marriage in a more charitable manner. Faith, in other words, will be lived out in specific ways and those ways can be very different among people and if the biblical examples I just gave are correctly interpreted, then what Jesus expects the interior framework of a given person's faith to be will be specific to the situation of the person involved.

The interior framework of faith cannot, in the end, be separated from faith. Faith is embedded in, and shaped by, an individual life and looks different for individual people. I heard a story of two friends listening to a "mediocre" sermon. When one friend turned to the other to criticize and make fun of the sermon, he noticed his friend's head bowed, tears rolling down his cheeks. Salvation doesn't come to all of us the same way. But perhaps we need to go further: to think not merely of different responses of faith but of alternative accounts of human access. Do we access the grace of God's salvation via a mental attitude one should take up (taking up faith, taking on hope, accepting forgiveness, feeling more compassionate)? Is it developing a deeper spiritual relationship with Jesus (praying more, trying to rely on the strength of the Holy Spirit)? Is it loving one's neighbor (selling all one has and giving to the poor, taking up a cause such as fighting sex slavery), accepting healing and becoming grateful for God's grace (such as the one out of ten lepers healed who returned to thank Jesus), or is it something else again? What I propose is that the holder of CSE, while often just listing one of these sorts of things (*personal* faith being the most favorite evangelical Protestant item) also builds into that one a combination of other things. Thus, a person who holds CSE may take a union of some of these—say having faith *and* accepting God's forgiveness—and then hold that union as the only means of access to the work of Christ. The main point for the holder of CSE is that she takes her list of human means of access and understands it as *jointly necessary and sufficient* to access the work of Christ.

The inclusivist, in contrast, will have a problem with the necessity claim (the sufficiency of individual components remaining unproblematic). My point is that so long as a Christian holds a union of some of the possibilities *as a union* and claims that that union is necessary for salvation, so far forth that person is a holder of CSE. The holder of CSE cannot make a disjunctive list of items. She can't say *either* have faith *or* love Jesus *or* love your neighbor *or* become Christ-like. That would make her an inclusivist. The holder of CSE must have a fused notion of the one (joint) thing one must do to be saved.

So there are two aspects to what I've been saying. First, the single access upheld by the holder of CSE is often a *fused* access where faith (or something else) enfolds other things, such as living morally, developing a good prayer life, etc. Second, each person has her own account of our human access to God, whether fused or simple. Where the accounts of distinct persons are different, the claim is still exclusive because each distinct person will claim that her own version extends to everyone else as necessary for salvation.

Let's consider the good Baptist folks I grew up with in church. I was taught that faith alone was the means to access Jesus's salvific life and work. Furthermore, I was taught that since everyone needs to hear and respond to Jesus' claims on his or her life that I should engage in evangelistic work—sharing the story of Jesus at every opportunity. As a result of this, I was concerned about how people who'd never heard the gospel message could be fairly treated since, indeed, one must have faith in Christ for salvation.

Setting the Salvific Stage

In other words, I was taught that having a "personal" faith in Christ was the necessary human means of access to Christ and that such faith had little to do salvifically with church, communion, baptism, or anything else connected to the church. Of course, one should do those things (go to church, take communion, be baptized) but only because they were one's task of obedience. They had nothing to do with accessing salvation for oneself. They were not, in fact, part of saving faith.

In contrast, consider a Roman Catholic who has committed a mortal sin. He is aware of his guilt before God, attends reconciliation on Saturday, confesses his sin to his priest, and receives forgiveness. He later joins the Eucharistic celebration, taking in the body and blood of Jesus as a means of grace. He has followed the teaching of his youth, engaging with the church through whom salvation comes as the very presence of Christ on earth. Does he feel, or would he say, that he has a *personal* faith in Jesus? Perhaps neither. If not, then would he meet the sort of access requirements I was raised with? One suspects the answer is "no." That, at least, was what I was taught as a youth myself. Roman Catholics (who were not, for the most part, thought of as Christians) were to be included among the objects of my Baptist evangelistic efforts.

This is a two-way street. If the Baptist asked the Catholic[3] whether he believed the Baptist was responding properly to God, surely he would say "no." Faith involves confession, receiving forgiveness via a priest, taking communion, and so forth. Hence there is a need in Roman Catholic theology for the introduction of baptism of desire and baptism by blood. Such things allow for many to be saved without going through the church *in fact*. Faith involves no such thing for the Baptist. She will suggest that one only needs to trust Jesus for salvation. Baptism and communion—even living a holy life before God—are not necessities for salvation. Functionally—and indeed, sometimes in clear teaching—our access to the gospel comes down to a singular but fused notion of human salvific access.

I want to quote at least one author who seems to hold a fairly strict access exclusivism. Consider the following: "Christian exclusivism, which has been the view of Reformed and Biblically orthodox churches through the centuries, is the teaching that (1) Jesus Christ is the only Savior, and (2) that it is essential for one to believe in Him in order to be saved. This view

---

3. This is especially true of pre-Vatican II Catholics, but can still be true today even though official Catholic teaching is more open. Nevertheless, the Catholic Church holds that in order for people to best or more fully respond to God, they should become Catholic and participate in the life of the Roman church.

is admirably set forth in the Westminster Shorter Catechism (Q. 21), the Westminster Confession of Faith (10:4; 14:2), and the Westminster Larger Catechism (Q. 60)."[4] The author, W. Gary Crampton, then quotes those texts. Here are the relevant parts.

> The only Redeemer of God's elect is the Lord Jesus Christ. Others, not elected, although they may be called by the ministry of the Word, and may have some common operations of the Spirit, yet they never truly come unto Christ, and therefore cannot be saved: Much less can men, not professing the Christian religion, be saved in any other way whatsoever, be they never so diligent to frame their lives according to the light of nature [general revelation], and the law of that religion they do profess. And, to assert and maintain that they may, is very pernicious, and to be detested. But the principal acts of saving faith are accepting, receiving, and resting upon Christ alone for justification, sanctification, and eternal life, by virtue of the covenant of grace. They who, having never heard the gospel, know not Jesus Christ, and believe not in Him, cannot be saved ... neither is their salvation in any other, but in Christ alone, who is the Savior only of His body the church.[5]

Here it is clear that access to the saving work of the gospel is limited to those who hear the word and believe it. The light of nature is not ever enough. But I'm interested more in the account of access itself, that is, what one must do to access the salvific work. Although still not as exclusively stated as it could be, the Westminster divines claim that one can only access the work of Christ via belief, *viz.*, by accepting, receiving, and resting upon Christ alone. Does Crampton (or the writers of the confessions) actually believe that there is only one way to access salvation? Certainly in the sense that one must believe in Christ. Now one might take the above passage to be fairly open-ended about what believing in Christ is, but it's not clear why we should take it thus. When asked a question such as "what must I do to be saved?" many Christians will give a fairly straightforward answer (as Crampton does, following the confessions), and when asked to clarify it, those same Christians will give an account according to their own (and/or their Christian community's) account of faith (in Crampton's case, a strongly Reformed view). So that there are true exclusivists of the sort I've been discussing may be hard to demonstrate in terms of finding official and detailed descriptions, but it is not hard to pin down when talking to the

---

4. Crampton, "Christian Exclusivism."
5. As quoted by Crampton in ibid.

average Christian. I believe that many Christians take their own model of faith based on interior structures and require it of others in practice if not in theory.

We might also use the term "naïve realist" as a replacement for "exclusivist." Here I have in mind something like the naïve realist in epistemology, who more or less believes what he sees (or more generally perceives). A coin held before the eyes is round. So goes common sense (and naïve realism). But when held out flat before the eyes so one views the edge, the coin is also rectangular. Which is it? The Christian naïve realist about salvation takes her own first impression as the only true account. But naïve realism is, on the face of it, a faulty way to think. Thinking realistically is perhaps a good way to think, but not in a *naïve* way. Yet we are often prone to naiveté when it comes to epistemological situations. The question is whether we need to be a little more circumspect in the way we talk about salvific access. Both the "round" and the "rectangular" description are correct of the coin, even if the one is most predominant in our everyday, less cautious talk. I propose the same is true of salvific access.

But whether we use the term "exclusivist" or "naïve realist," it seems safe to say that plenty of everyday lay Christians *appear* to hold such a view or act as if they do, thus having a sort of functional belief in exclusivism. When asked, one may receive a quick response: in order to be saved, you must do such-and-so. But it is not just lay people who hold the view. A good number of local churches *teach* that unless one comes, for example, to trust Jesus Christ for one's salvation, one is going to hell. If asked what it means to "trust Jesus," one is told: recognize your sin, repent of it, ask Jesus to forgive it, and turn to Christ in belief (trust). There is no other means by which the work of Christ can ever be applied to people, even those who, through no fault of their own, have never even heard of Jesus, let alone the larger message of Christian salvation.

Intellectuals perhaps tend to ignore such churches, sometimes writing them off as "fundamentalist." Nevertheless, such churches promote CSE, although they don't typically call it that. Perhaps they are in the minority and as such they are not holding views consonant with the larger Christian church. Perhaps, indeed, very few churches actually *teach* CSE. Furthermore, some intellectuals will admit the mere sociological point that some churches do teach CSE and that some lay people believe it but then go on to note that this has nothing of interest to say to a philosophy of the Christian faith. Philosophy should worry about what is actually taught in the Christian *tradition* rather than what might be taken as rather aberrant beliefs found among the masses. Philosophers shouldn't bother since we have enough on our hands to concern us with the larger tradition. We can thus ignore the mere sociology of lay people. The church should be left to do its job, which would include teaching its parishioners better doctrine.

Such an approach misses important aspects of the actual lives of believers and overlooks features of the "tradition" that ought not to be overlooked. Philosophy is not just about theory, or at least it shouldn't be. It should also be about helping people become more wise, more mature, even more (intellectually and spiritually) healthy. Furthermore, the notion of "tradition" can be a rather sloppy one. Of course, there is the sense of tradition that points to the church councils. There is also the sense of tradition that points to what a particular church body has done—say the Roman Catholic Church or one Baptist association or another. There is also the Reformed tradition and the Armenian tradition. And so on. Certainly the fact that some churches have in the past taught and today continue to teach that there is a singular means of accessing the work of Christ is part of the "tradition" of the broader church. On top of that, how the broader culture, at least in America, views the teaching of the Christian tradition should play in here. The church is often viewed as overly narrow in approach to how humans can relate well to God, a point reflected in the commonly heard "I am spiritual, but I don't think much of organized religion."

But it is not, in fact, just local churches that hold to CSE or something very close to it. I've already quoted W. Gary Crampton and the Reformed confessions to which he points. But consider as well the following from the Southern Baptist Convention: "Salvation involves the redemption of the whole man, and is offered freely to all who accept Jesus Christ as Lord and Saviour, who by His own blood obtained eternal redemption for the believer. In its broadest sense salvation includes regeneration, justification, sanctification, and glorification. *There is no salvation apart from personal faith in Jesus Christ as Lord.*"[6]

Of course, as I noted above in mentioning Crampton's point of view, the notion of *personal faith* could be quite broad. One supposes there are "sawdust trail" sorts of conversion where one "gives one's heart to Jesus" in a momentary decision, thereby bringing about (or expressing one's new) personal faith. There are also Roman Catholic "conversions" that come over time by participating in the Eucharist and other sacraments. Both sorts of

---

6. Southern Baptist Convention, "Basic Beliefs." Italics mine.

"conversion" could—and, I think, *should*—be described as bringing about personal faith. No doubt there are others as well. I won't explore other alternatives here, but the general view is exclusivist in terms not only of the basis of salvation (the work of Christ) but in terms of human access. One *must* have personal faith in Jesus Christ as Lord. Just how broad this notion of faith is, of course, an open question. But presumably it's not too open. One who had never heard of Jesus and perhaps didn't believe in God at all but who lived an exemplary good life would not be described as having personal faith in Jesus in the relevant sense. Being good is not the same as having faith—all our righteousness is as filthy rags, one might note. To be exclusivist about human access to God's salvation, one must think there are some limits on what "personal faith" comes to.

Could CSE be the teaching of Scripture? I've introduced the idea of fused notions of access. Fused notions are no less unique or singular than unfused notions. What if the Scripture itself teaches that "faith" is a fused notion? Perhaps as we read the New Testament we should be thinking about all the ways presented to access the work of Christ and make a very long list of items all of which together are necessary. We would then need to add, perhaps, the means of access that have accrued over the years within various church histories—Roman Catholic, Orthodox, Lutheran, etc. Of course, that makes accessing the work of Jesus very difficult. To have faith would then involve a good many things. But such a move might also create contradictions within the description of the fused notion of access. Perhaps we simply can't put together the Baptist notion with the Catholic notion.

Even if we could, we simply can't do everything and that can create one sort of existential issue for a person. Spiritual directors see this sort of crisis regularly. Christians come for help in sorting out the guilt they feel in not doing enough for God. They feel pulled and stretched in too many directions. Go to church, work with the poor, raise my children, pray, give generously. Sometimes, of course, that is merely the stress of living our lives. But when these things are thought of as part-and-parcel of having faith, they can turn into faith-jeopardizing situations.

In response to that enormous demand, what we do typically is winnow all the examples and sayings of Jesus, Paul, Peter, and the others to get the *kernel* of human access. We can summarize this approach with Jesus' saying, "Come, follow me." But what does following Jesus entail? In answer, one typically specifies with some particular thing or other from the original list. We often do the same thing with "have faith in Jesus and his work." We then step into a specific version of what that faith ought to look like. Here our tendency to speak in Christian sound bites is a problem. Sometimes our practice of the Christian faith gets over-simplified with the vague "have faith" or "follow Jesus." If not left there, we go on to specify what one of those suggestions should look like and we start to sound like we hold CSE with a fused account of human access. So we are either too vague or too specific. The difficulty comes down to the *necessity* of a particular access, no matter what it is. So the question may be whether any particular thing (or fused group of things) one can do is necessary or are there a variety of means (some of which we may not even be aware of) that are sufficient, no particular one of which is necessary *per se*.

It is often in the interpretive process of many Christians that the "official" teaching of a church focuses down functionally to be quite narrow. Would, for example, living the faithful life of a Roman Catholic express the life of Baptist-style faith, especially where the Roman church emphasizes the veneration of Mary? While some evangelical Christians can see their way to accepting Roman Catholics as fellow followers of Jesus, many do not. Having taught at an evangelical Christian university for a large number of years, I can personally bear witness to the substantial resistance many evangelical students (and their parents) have to the notion that the Roman Catholic way of faith is a true way of faith. Once again, function is not official teaching, but function often tells us what the *de facto* teaching is taken, and hence believed, to be.

But sometimes even the official teaching seems to rule out people from salvation who, it seems, should attain it, at least from a human perspective. I heard an account of a monk who spent his entire adult life not believing in any apparent way in the work of Jesus and, in fact, took himself to lack not only trust but belief in God. He simply did not have the attitudinal aspect of belief—the sort of "luminous glow" that attaches to propositions when we believe them, and he certainly didn't have the rich attitude of trust toward Christ. In short, he lacked faith even though he wanted very much to have faith. Nevertheless, he regularly performed his duties, reciting his prayers, participating in the life of the community and so forth. When asked why he continued on in this fairly difficult life, he replied only that he very much wished to have faith and belief in God and the work of Christ but he just didn't. He hoped, however, that his hope that the Gospel accounts were true would be enough. God, apparently, hadn't given this monk the gift of faith as we might typically understand it. One wonders whether, according to the

Baptist statement of faith, this monk had accessed the salvation provided by God.

A related, but different story is from my own life. One of my university professors in philosophy told me that he would really like to be a person of faith—he wished he was—but he just didn't have faith. Now his response, unlike the monk, was not to do anything about what he wished. He didn't attend church or anything of the sort. He just wished he could have faith but didn't. Perhaps my professor differed from the monk in that the monk had hope whereas my professor only wished. A different friend of mine told me that he, too, wanted to be a Christian. He went forward at an altar call at a Billy Graham crusade and prayed with someone to receive Christ into his life. My friend experienced nothing, nothing beyond a desire to be a Christian. He was, he told me, disappointed, but he couldn't bring himself to believe without any sort of attending experience.

Now in these last couple of cases, it appears that neither the typical Roman Catholic nor the typical Baptist account of human salvific access would apply. Neither my professor nor my friend had faith and only one tried to obtain it (at the Billy Graham crusade). Neither one went much beyond the surface at trying to obtain faith. They didn't join a monastery, attend church, get baptized, go to Bible studies or anything remotely Christian. They would, it seems, both fail the human access test of virtually any Christian tradition. Perhaps, then, they just weren't saved. But the point is, functionally many in the church would say that such folk are clearly outside the faith, no matter how much they wanted to be inside. Functionally, that is CSE in operation.

So far forth, my discussion has been an "internal" one; that is, I've been concerned to talk about various criteria for human access to the Christian salvific ontology—the life and work of Jesus. But often the concern is not so much which means is right within the church but how we should think of applying the access criteria to those outside the church. The latter, of course, depends upon the former. Is there some way to include within the salvific circle those of other faiths, those who've never heard the gospel, or those who are simply not religious at all?

II

Let's turn briefly to inclusivism and pluralism. Salvific religious pluralism (SRP), in stark contrast to CSE, often does not hold a metaphysical realism or a monistic salvific ontology, or a single means of human access. SRP comes in a wide variety of shapes and forms and I'll return below to describe it in some more detail. What I want to note here is that often the driving force behind a move to SRP for a person who starts out life as a CSE Christian[7] is the sense that one does not want to be unfair or judgmental toward those of other religious faiths or practices. Those who find CSE untenable sometimes see no middle ground between CSE and SRP and hence move all the way to SRP. In doing so, however, many Christians feel they are losing something of value; they feel they have lost the truth of the faith. Some folk, however, may not see the choice between CSE and SRP as an either/or and they come to an island in the middle of the river. Not wanting to lose the truth claims of the Christian faith but wanting to include those of other faiths, they move to Christian salvific inclusivism (CSI). CSI holds 1 and 2, but modifies 3.

> 3* More than one means can grant access to the proper salvific relationship to God through Jesus Christ and those means are disjunctively necessary and sufficient.

In the most conservative of the inclusivist options, the list of means is expanded only modestly. The means are often thought to be fundamentally the same as are found referred to in 3 (typically tied to the hearing of special revelation) with the addition of a means of access due to natural revelation. For example, once having heard of the special revelation of God in Jesus Christ, one can take up faith in Jesus as one's Savior and Lord. For those who have never heard of the special revelation of God in Jesus Christ (or the Christian Scriptures more generally) the light of natural revelation is sufficient to provide grounds for access to salvation. The light of natural revelation gives one enough to turn toward the truth, but the truth is perhaps quite vaguely understood. Romans 1:18–23 says:

> For the wrath of God is revealed from heaven against all ungodliness and wickedness of those who by their wickedness suppress the truth. For what can be known about God is plain to them, because God has shown it to them. Ever since the creation of the

---

7. There are, of course, religious pluralists who hold to pluralism because it is taught as one aspect of their religion. Advaita Vedanta Hindus come to mind. All religious descriptions are, so to speak, mythological on the ground and one can move to *moksha* through any religious description. My main concern here is for Christians, for Christianity appears to have an exclusivism built into it and many are raised with that exclusivism in the background, if not the foreground, of their understanding of the faith.

world his eternal power and divine nature, invisible though they are, have been understood and seen through the things he has made. So they are without excuse; for though they knew God, they did not honor him as God or give thanks to him, but they became futile in their thinking, and their senseless minds were darkened. Claiming to be wise, they became fools; and they exchanged the glory of the immortal God for images resembling a mortal human being or birds or four-footed animals or reptiles.

Here we find one version of the light of nature. According to Paul, nature teaches all of us that God is and that God has eternal power and a divine nature. This is enough to render humans without excuse before God for their wickedness. This passage is a negative one, of course, noting that people have turned away from the information given in the light of nature and exchanged the glory of the immortal God for images of mortal things. Nevertheless, an inclusivist can say that the light of nature is present and some people will or can turn toward the light and, presumably, therefore be saved. What turning toward the light comes to is, however, less than clear. Given the Scripture just quoted, it appears one would at least believe in God based on natural revelation. Is that enough? Or does one have to trust God too? Or does one have to trust God in such a way to avoid idol worship, thus avoiding a wicked suppression of truth? It at least appears from this passage that those of religions other than Christianity may very well be excluded insofar as they are suppressing the truth about God by exchanging the glory of God for idols.[8] An inclusivism based on such a view is quite narrow. But it has this feature, *viz.*, that 1 and 2 are still held to be true. Only 3 is modified, even if in a narrow sense.

But inclusivism can come in wider forms as well. One could, for example, take the gospel of the light of nature more widely than in the previous interpretation of Romans 1. Rather than saying that those of religions other than Christianity are makers of idols, one could say that, given the light they have, they are thinking of God in the best way they can and are turning, thereby, to the source of the light they have. The content of their beliefs would be largely wrong, one supposes. However, they are being faithful followers of the source of the light, even though they do not know

---

8. I think a much better reading of this text is that Paul's intent is to show how we are all living in sin and therefore without excuse before God. It is not so much teaching that followers of non-Christian religions are not saved *because* they worship idols. His point is that there is enough light in the natural order that we are responsible for our actions, rather than a point about salvation itself.

the truth about that source. Here the emphasis is not on proper belief-content or even the reality behind one's salvific impulses. It is, instead, on the human response. Does this person *want* to be saved, even though the person, perhaps, doesn't really know what salvation is?

A clearer and more sophisticated version of inclusivism is the following one. CSI works by appealing to direct reference as a means of referring to God. To my knowledge the grounds for this were first formally laid out by William Alston.[9] He suggests that a person might refer to Christ or Christ's work via direct reference, *even when one is quite mistaken about the description of Christ*. A Buddhist, for instance, may refer to Christ when, for example, talking about enlightenment, even though a description of enlightenment will not accurately describe Jesus. An inclusivist might say that a Buddhist refers to Christ and is, therefore, saved by Christ. The Buddhist simply doesn't know it. Here, one supposes, the light of natural revelation results in taking the world in such a way that while appearing incompatible with the Christian story is not actually incompatible because salvation occurs through a referential mechanism quite outside the saved person's knowledge. Thus, one could be an inclusivist about salvific access (one can access the work of Christ in many ways, even if one doesn't know one is doing so) but an exclusivist about the ontological basis of salvation (the work of Christ) and therefore an exclusivist about the truth of the gospel.

Let me return to SRP. Pluralism in this context comes in a variety of forms, but typically denies each of 1, 2, and 3, or at least aspects of them. While SRP need not deny, for example, that the natural order is truly described only one way, the salvific order is something else again.[10] Not only is there more than one means of accessing salvation on the human side, but the divine (or ultimate reality) side of the equation can be truly described more than one way or, perhaps, mythically described more than one way. Buddhism, Hinduism, Christianity, etc., are all true or, if not all true literally, all true mythically. All lead to salvation, although perhaps not to the salvation that any of the actual religions literally describe. But mythical or phenomenological descriptions give us a place to live out our religious lives while noumenally the nature of salvation is beyond our ken. One can think of John Hick's work in these terms and, in some ways, Advaita

---

9. Alston, "Referring."

10. One could, of course, be an antirealist all the way through and hence antirealist about religious claims as well as claims about the natural order. Such a view would have the same problems as those discussed in the text.

Vedanta Hindusim.[11] The varieties of SRP are wide and it is not my purpose to describe or evaluate them in any detail. However, there are some general considerations that go into my rejecting them. First, some versions of SRP rely on antirealist accounts of truth (epistemic or perhaps deflationary[12]) as well as a global antirealist metaphysics in regard to religious subjects. As will eventually become clear, I hold what I call an *ir*realistic metaphysic (a description I use to distinguish it from global *anti*realisms). But my view is not irrealistic all the way down on religious matters and hence is not global. I reject global antirealism when it comes not only to religious subjects but to the whole order of reality. I think good grounds exist philosophically to reject globally antirealist views and, insofar as SRP relies on those positions, good grounds to reject SRP.

Two reasons I reject truly global antirealist metaphysics are because they tend to create various infinite regress problems and they seem to grant human beings far too much creative power, power it seems we just don't have.[13] Thus, the irrealism I propose is not as radical as global antirealism. In fact, it requires the existence and creative activity of God to side-step the infinite regress issues often involved in antirealism. Nevertheless, it is a *nearly* global irrealism, not merely in the field of religion, but about everything.

But not all SRPs rely on global metaphysical antirealisms. Those which do not, fall prey to another criticism. That is, insofar as SRP undermines the average believer/practitioner's actual way of life (one's trust, for example, in Jesus or one's approach to enlightenment or one's seeking for moksha), SRP does the religious believer/practitioner few favors. Eventually, discovering that one's own religious approach to salvific reality is merely "mythical" has a tendency to undermine one's motivation to continue to practice one's belief. In this regard, note how many Christian students give up their faith

---

11. See Hick, *Interpretation of Religion*. Advaita Vedanta Hinduism is perhaps a religious view itself, but can also be taken as a philosophical view about religion. Here complications abound, but fortunately I need not explore those here.

12. A deflationary theory of truth says, in short, that to say something is true is just a linguistic way of emphasizing a claim. One asserts that what one says is true, thereby emphasizing it, but there is no deep theory underpinning such claims. An epistemic theory of truth, in short, says that our epistemological positions contribute to that fact that a proposition is true. A realist theory denies both those positions suggesting that there is more to truth than a sort of emphasis of language (and that there can be a "deep theory") as well saying that our epistemic situation does not in any way make a proposition true.

13. For more on this, see McLeod-Harrison, "God and (Nearly) Global" and Alston, *A Sensible Metaphysical Realism*.

as they attend universities and discover that their non-Christian religious neighbor has good grounds for her belief and practice. I explore and describe that issue in more detail elsewhere.[14] For the most part, religious believers/practitioners take their beliefs to be true and generally grounded in what they take to be real and largely independent of human noetic creativity. The view I propose below avoids this challenge because the God who underlies the view is not at the divine core dependent upon human noetic contributions from humans. (I'll explain "the divine core" below.) For all of that, my goal in this essay does not include an evaluation of SRP. Rather, I begin with the Christian account of the world and try to make sense of it being both true and inclusive.[15]

CSI, in contrast to many versions of SRP, is usually given account as holding a realist metaphysic and a realist theory of truth (often a correspondence theory), which are the same positions (typically) underlying CSE. While I accept a realist account of truth, I reject the correspondence theory and I further believe that the realist metaphysic or parts of it are questionable. But if that metaphysic is itself faulty, another alternative is needed. What follows proposes an alternative to SRP, CSI, and CSE that allows traditional Christianity to be true and yet rejects the faulty metaphysical views standing behind both CSE and CSI on the one hand and SRP on the other. That is, it rejects metaphysical realism and global metaphysical antirealism for religious subjects respectively.

The good news is, there is a way of being an inclusivist while rejecting a strict metaphysical realism and one can do so without losing the core of Christian orthodoxy. It is important to note that that alternative does not entail moving all the way from metaphysical realism to global antirealism and the off-stage SRP attending to it, a pluralism that many traditional Christians are concerned to reject. In other words, the argument I propose does not reject the notion that the Christian God exists independent of human noetic work, at least at the divine core. God is the ultimate creator,

---

14. See McLeod-Harrison, *Repairing Eden*.

15. Here I must add something again about Advaita Vedanta Hinduism. One raised in that tradition will not be thrown off her religious commitment when finding other religions claiming to be true. She already has a framework for including the religious worldviews of others. However, there may be other issues embedded in Advaita that undermines the view itself, problems similar to those John Hick faces. For example, what is the content of the actual belief of one holding to Advaita? It appears mostly a negative account of reality, an account of which we can say very little. What role does belief play, if any? Can we say, in our ignorance, that we have any sort of accurate description of Brahman? Again, I won't pursue the issues here any further.

not humans. Nor does it reject a realist (albeit minimalist) theory of truth. However, it is not committed to a full-orbed correspondence theory of truth either. What follows, in short, is merely an application of theistic irrealism to Christian salvation. I call the resulting view "Christian salvific expansivism" to distinguish it from the more standard understandings of CSI.

Chapter 2

On Being the Literal Image of God

Suppose two painters go to northern California, set up their easels, and paint images of Mt. Shasta. While there is a very good chance the two paintings will appear similar, sharing certain properties, they need not. Suppose one painter is a realist and his painting "looks like the mountain" whereas the other painter is a cubist and her painting looks (virtually) nothing like the mountain. Both, however, label their paintings "Mt. Shasta at Morning Light" and both mean their labels to be taken literally. The resulting paintings, although both images of Mt. Shasta, appear to share little in common. It is hard to see how any property of one is a property of the other except at a trivial level (say, both are painted on canvass, with oils, and the like). One might be black and grey, portraying various angles of the mountain (the cubist) and the other (the realist) might be bright red and orange, portraying a "true to life" single angle, and so forth. Images are not only unique but sometimes hardly rooted in "the way things are."

It's perhaps curious then, that when we think of humans as the image of God, we typically don't think of uniqueness. If we think of the image of God in terms of pictures at all (which isn't, I think, common), we tend to think of cookie-cutter images, each of us being enough like God that we are recognizably the same. The notion of cookie-cutter images is then standardly understood in (traditional) Christian thinking by taking a Platonic approach to what it is to be human. It thus cashes out the nature of humanity in terms of (essential) properties, such as rationality, emotional richness, volition, and spirituality.¹ Frequently, in other words, Christian theology takes the image-of-God language of Scripture as mere metaphor for something more important. That is, the term "image" is taken to need reduction to some other term or terms that are literal. I want to challenge that approach.

I challenge the status quo because if we consider the vast differences in personality and experience among humans, it seems obvious that our individual uniquenesses are, in important ways, central to what we are as individuals. Consequently, our uniquenesses are also central to salvation. What I need to be saved from of course overlaps with what you need to be saved from, but what I need to be saved from is also unique to me. My sin is *my* sin, not yours; my life is *my* life, not yours. A model of the image of God that allows both for our commonalities and our uniquenesses will be more true to our experience than the standard commonalities approach.

If, in fact, human access to salvation is protean, as I suggest below, then one might wonder how salvation can be provided universally by the work of one (divine-)human Jesus? How does the image of God play into the pluralistic account of salvific access provided thus far?

Section I suggests some reasons why Christian theologians are reluctant to take the image-of-God language of Scripture too literally. Sections II–IV describe three ways of understanding the term "image," each relevant to the image of God. Section V applies the results of II–IV to the theological context of humans made in the divine image. Section VI reflects briefly on sin and salvation.

I

Why don't we take the phrase "image of God" as literal? For one thing, images can be wildly different from one another as noted in the first paragraph and that seems incongruent with the role the notion of the image of God plays in Christian theology and philosophy. If we eschew taking the image language as literal, it is easier for Christian philosophers and theologians to suggest that we have common ground with our secular colleagues. We can say, for example, that humans are what we are because of some set of

---

1. The non-physical properties that might be found on the list of essential properties is quite long. Besides those mentioned in the text, one could include knowledge, moral sensibility, power, wisdom, and others. I'll stick to the list I provided in the text, but it is not meant to be exclusive or exhaustive.

necessary properties by which we are all united. This sort of view grounds moral obligation and the possibility of universal virtues. But more importantly for our purposes here, the power of the essentialist reading of the image language plays right into how we understand two major Christian doctrines: sin and salvation.

The common nature of humanity roots the doctrine of sin. We are all born into sin because we share the same nature as Adam and Eve. When they fell, we fell. Whatever sin did to us, the fact that we all have the same essential properties is what allows sin to be passed from one to the other down through history.[2] The fact that we all have the image of God (in the form of essential properties) supports the doctrine of original sin. That shared nature is a corrupted nature passed along generationally.

The doctrine of salvation through Christ also finds its roots in taking the image of God to be something we all share. Since Christ is human he also is made in the image of God. His image, however, is without sin. Hence Christ can save us by his life, death, and resurrection, effectively answering the question *cur deus homo*? Christ takes on the image of God, understood as a set of essential properties, and works in reverse what we find in the doctrine of sin. Through one person, Adam, sin enters the world, through one person, Jesus, sin is overcome. What Adam corrupted Jesus uncorrupts and because we are made in the image of God—for we share the same essential properties—sin can be overcome by the perfect life and sacrifice of Christ.

The advantage of having a shared, essential human nature seems thus to be sewn up in a nice, neat theological package. Without a shared human essence, it's not clear how sin could be original or how Christ could save us. In other words, it's not clear how taking the image-of-God language of the Scriptures as anything but metaphorical can provide for either of these theological necessities. We tend to think images are mere copies (a point I'll discuss further below) and copies are not related to one another in a sophisticated-enough way philosophically to ground these two central doctrines. Since two copies of the same original can be substantially different, if we take the image-of-God language as literal it looks as though perhaps nothing unites us essentially. Each of us is a mere copy of God (some better, one might suppose, some worse). So while the image-of-God language

---

2. Curiously, being sinful is not one of the essential properties of humans, otherwise we could never be freed from it. While it seems clear that sin affected the image of God in us negatively, how that is related to essential properties is less than clear. That is a topic I'll not enter here, but it seems very much worth exploring.

lends itself well to pointing out the uniqueness of the human individual it may not point toward the commonality of all the members of the race. Insofar as we are unique creations of God we run the risk of disconnecting humans one from the other and perhaps from Jesus himself. The potential uniqueness of images would tend to undermine the unity of human persons if we were to be literal images of God.

I propose that Christian theologians and philosophers are often beguiled by two notions. First, the long-standing cultural assumption rooted in Plato's powerful observation that when X copies Y, X is less real than Y. X *as an image* thus misleads us by taking us away from truth and toward error. Hence, the idea that humans are made in the image of God must be a metaphor for something else, something philosophers and theologians can grapple with, something about which true or universal things can be said. Perhaps something similar is behind the ancient prohibition against making images of God or perhaps against any images at all. "You shall not make for yourself an idol, whether in the form of anything that is in heaven above, or that is on the earth beneath, or that is in the water under the earth. You shall not bow down to them or worship them" (Exod 20:4–5a). Perhaps Moses would have agreed with Plato about images. But if images mislead, somehow pulling on our emotions rather than our reason, philosophy and theology somehow gets at reality and truth. So thought Plato and maybe Moses.[3]

The second beguiling notion is that since God is a spirit rather than a body, and since humans are bodies, or have bodies, the image of God in humans cannot be bodily. The image of God must be non-material. Hence, rationality, emotional richness, volition, and spirituality are likely candidates for what Scripture means when it's talking about the image of God. The image of God cannot be our bodies. A related factor feeding this sort of argument is also Greek, viz., that what is truly valuable is not the body but the soul. If God made us in the divine image, it must be a spiritual image, matter being somewhat suspect. No matter how much theologians have tried to correct this notion, it is still very much with us.

I argue below that understanding the image-of-God language more literally can, in fact, make sense of the doctrines of sin and salvation, both of which rely on properties being shared among humans. Our being

---

3. Of course, the context of the prohibition against images in Moses is far more complicated than I've indicated. Indeed, it may be that no image was to be made in order to worship it or because we humans already are the image of God or perhaps for some other reason.

individual images of God does not rule out our having essential properties that we share in common and thus unite us as children of God. Indeed, I suggest that being unique is, in fact, one of the essential properties God gives to us. My argument that our individual uniquenesses are the image of God also has the result that we have theological grounds for our (fairly recent cultural) celebratory emphasis on diversity and uniqueness. Finally, the shift in emphasis developed here helps to make sense out of the intuition that our uniqueness as individuals makes us valuable. Even though this intuition is widely held (at least in popular culture) it is not widely defended or explained in either theology or philosophy. By approaching the notion of the image of God as the source of my being unique, my moral and spiritual value can be grounded in what is truly special about me and not merely the fact that you, I, and all of us together are alike "under the skin."

II

What does the term "image" mean? Many things, lexically. One dictionary lists seventeen entries, both nouns and verbs. I discuss only three. One common understanding of image depends on a particular structure and relationship. Typically there is a (pre-existing) entity that something else copies, resembles, or represents. I'll call this the "object/image dichotomy" and images that result from it "dichotomous images." Typically, this sort of imaging involves a physical image of another physical thing.

Often we talk about such imaging in terms of there first being something real and then an image of it. This pattern of talk has created much havoc in the way we think about images, beginning with Plato's observation that the arts merely copy what is real and are, therefore, less real and, therefore, misleading. Art, suggests Plato, is simply not reality, but a copy of it, from which ensues the entire philosophy vs. poetry debate. In response it is important to note that an image, although typically copying, resembling, or representing another real thing, is still, itself, *a real thing*. Twentieth century art and art theory picks up this theme.[4]

The problem perhaps originates with the notion of copying. In general terms, to copy X implies that X already exists (or at least did exist). There is a temporal ordering that typically attaches to copying. The original object comes first and the copied image second. However, not all images have that sort of structure. Y can resemble X without X having come first temporally.

4. See for example discussions by Danto, *The Transfiguration*.

Y and X merely have to be alike in some feature or other. Of course, the more alike two things are, the more likely the judgment will be made that the two things resemble one another, and certainly the better the copy, the more the copy resembles the original.

Representation need not imply resemblance or copying. Virtually anything could represent some other thing, given the right circumstances. A rock can represent, for example, the Queen of England, or the Queen of England can represent a country, or a country represent freedom. So we really have two sorts of dichotomous images: copy and representational. The only common rule between the two seems to be that if X represents or copies Y, then X and Y cannot be numerically identical. There are exceptions, perhaps. One can represent oneself in a courtroom in lieu of hiring a lawyer. That seems to be something of an anomaly however, deriving from the fact that one typically has a lawyer represent one under legal circumstances. We may simply use the term "represent" here because one typically has a representative. In fact, however, I believe these sorts of cases involve imaging of another sort, to which I return in section IV.

With a dichotomous image we are dealing with two real things whose relationship includes a more or less complex sort of logical dependency. Fundamentally, the relationship is not causal in the sense that when X copies or represents Y, Y brought X into being. In the case of copies, however, without Y's existence (now or in the past), X couldn't be a copy of Y. Yet insofar as X copies Y, Y is causally relevant for at least some of the features of X, viz., those features X and Y have in common. I'll say that if X copies Y, Y is present to a causal chain of events such that, without Y being present to the chain, X would not copy Y. This is not true with resemblances. X can resemble Y without Y being present to the causal chain that brings X about. The same is true in the opposite direction as well. That is, if Y resembles X, X need not be present to the causal chain that brings Y about. In other words, X and Y can resemble each other without the resemblance having anything to do with a mutual or overlapping history. Not so with copies. If X copies Y, there is a mutual or overlapping history. Finally, any and all copy relationships involve resemblance, but not all resemblances involve copies.

When X represents Y, however, there is even less of a logical connection. X can represent Y just by my saying that it does, as when I pick up a rock, set it on the table, and say that it represents (or is) the Queen of England. Representations are rooted in social or cultural relationships rather than any historical presence of the object to the representation. Often, of course, things that represent also copy or resemble the things being represented, but they need not. However, when X copies Y, X (the image) can standardly (although not necessarily) be thought to represent (the object) Y.

Also, while standardly X's copying Y does not include Y being the cause of X, it can. A picture of an apple is not caused by an apple. However, an artist can sketch herself, thereby copying herself and as such is both the causal source of the image as well as the object in the causal chain in which the shared features of the object and image are rooted. Here, so to speak, the picture of the apple *is* caused by the apple. In relation to this, cases of copying always involve intentionality, at least with artifacts. One must set out to copy something. Hence something's being a copy of another is not accidental or arbitrary. A piece of driftwood on the beach can resemble a person, but it doesn't copy a person. That is why an artist can copy herself and be the causal source of the copy. The history of a copy includes the intentional making of a copy whereas the history of a resembling image need not include intentional making at all.

With natural objects, at least those that fall into natural kinds, intentionality may not, and typically is not, involved. But information is shared from object to image. In natural reproduction, a mother lion gives birth to offspring which are copies of the mother. Here genetic coding carries the information for the copy and the mother (and father) are causes of the copy, as well as present to the causal chain. So in copies, whether artifactual or natural, information sharing occurs from object to copy.

Representation is similar to copying in regard to intentionality. It requires the intentional "making" of a representation. At some point, someone intends that X represents Y. While perhaps X might come to represent Y via a lost history (where no one can remember how one object came to represent another—say X marking the spot on a map where the treasure is: why not a T, for example?), there is still an intentional acceptance of X representing Y. Resemblance alone seems to be independent of our intending one thing to resemble another or even independent of informational sharing.

Let's consider briefly how images are related to some other mental processes that generate them. There are, for example, images that seem to "come out of one's head." Such images don't seem to copy another *actual* physical entity. Here we must be careful, for even images that do come "out of one's head" may still copy some other (physical) thing or at least something based on physical things. One's idea of an apple derives from having seen apples, and if an artist has never seen an apple, but merely had an apple described to her, her idea of an apple will ultimately be based on someone's having seen one. There are complications here that I need not attend to in detail, but should be mentioned. One's idea of an apple might be a very "visual" idea. That is, some people are quite adept at conjuring up a (mental) image in their minds and then are able to draw what they see with their "mind's eye." Those mental images, one might say, create a "virtual" reality that is then copied in the physical image (drawing, painting, sculpture, etc.). Sometimes one hears artists say "that's what I was seeing, that's what I wanted to draw" only after the sketch is on the paper but where, in fact, they did not have a model (physically) in front of them.

Others don't, apparently, think in pictures, but rather think fundamentally in words or concepts. Such a person might think "I'll draw an apple" and not, in fact, conjure up a virtual mental image of an apple but just have what might be thought of (in philosopher's jargon) as a "mental representation" of an apple. That last phrase, "mental representation" (that could, of course, include what I just called "virtual mental image") is a loaded one philosophically and I'm going to by-pass it as a distraction from my main point. Let's just say that in any (physical) image-making, the image is always mediated by the mind or its ideas or thoughts. Typically there is a physical object (or some idea based on physical objects) that falls on the "object" side of the object/image dichotomy and even though that is mediated through ideas or thoughts, the resulting (physical) image is an image of another physical object or thoughts derived from experiencing physical objects. That is true even where one "makes up" a physical object to then image. The last thought allows for fictional objects to be imaged as dichotomous images. For example, one could dichotomously image a fruit from the planet Zorb, something no human has ever seen before. Nevertheless, it would be "constructed" out of what other physical things look like—shapes, sizes, colors, etc. As Descartes notes, even the (physical) things I dream about borrow from (physical) things I've experienced.

The last two paragraphs are related to copies, but less clearly to resemblances. One can discover resemblances in nature without there being any corresponding creatively derivative work in the mind's eye.[5] It remains, of course, that the mind is doing some work in noting the resemblances. The

---

5. Here I'm setting aside the creative mental work that may go on in recognizing resemblances.

same is true where X represents Y. No mental imaging of the sort required in copying is needed, yet there is clearly mental work going on that links X with Y. In noting resemblances, one mentally compares the two objects. In representations, however, one must recognize a cultural "announcement" (or make one) of X representing Y. Of course, it may make it easier for us to recognize that X represents Y if, in fact, X resembles Y in some way, but X need not resemble Y to represent.[6]

Many times when we use the term "image" we have something like dichotomous images in mind. The limiting factor in the discussion thus far is the emphasis on the physical. While many images are physical, not all are. That some images are not physical is most certainly true in representations, where both physical and non-physical entities can represent either physical or non-physical things. The flag can represent courage, courage can represent the best in humanity, my thought about my mother can represent my mother, and finally, a stone, the Queen. What of copies? We say things like "his thought pattern copies Einstein's, with such and so difference." Do such dichotomous images follow the same patterns as those with physical objects? It appears so. Copying involves the necessity of the object being present to the causal chain that leads to the image, whereas resemblance need not. Representational imaging is a sort of social construct not rooted in copies or resemblance.

In summary, dichotomous images can be physical and non-physical but come in two sorts: copies and representations. Copies involve the presence of the object to the causal chain leading to the image and representations involve a decisional aspect of someone denoting that X represents Y even where neither copying nor resemblance is present.

III

I turn now to a second sort of image. Although not as common as the first one, there is a use of "image" that, if you will, carries its object with it. In

---

6. It is also worth noting that lots of things besides images are related in similar ways to ideas in the same way that copies are related to ideas. Cars, computers, and apple pies, for example. Although we sometimes refer to such things as images—as when, for example, we say the 1959 Cadillac is the image of post-war, American self-congratulation—typically we don't call cars "images." The process of making a car involves images, of course—sketches of prototypes, for example. However, that is art and often it is only art that draws out the term "image" for us. Of course, art covers a lot of territory.

this sense to be an image is to be an example of, the epitome of, or to typify.[7] For instance, we might say that Joe is the image of a football player or Mary is the image of a CEO. What this sense of image picks out depends a good deal on the tone of voice with which judgments about it are expressed. Both these examples can suggest a caricature of the sort of object under consideration. "Mary is the image of a CEO" could be pejorative, suggesting a negative picture not only of Mary, but of CEOs in general. Similarly "Joe is the image of a football player" could suggest a negative picture of football players and Joe as well. Or both could be positive. Mary or Joe could image the best of being a CEO or a football player, where being a CEO or a ball player are considered good things in their own right. In both the positive and the negative versions, however, what is meant depends further on the distinctions among examples, epitomes, and typifications.

To say X is *typical* of the set of Ys is often to say that X's properties are the properties commonly found attached to Ys. To say X is an *example* of the set of Ys is often to say the same sort of thing—X's properties are what are commonly found among Ys—but to be typical implies a stricter account, for what is typical of a set would not normally be capable of being a poor example of the set, whereas a mere example could be a poor example. Finally, for X to *epitomize* the set of Ys seems somewhat stronger than either being an example or being typical. To epitomize often picks out what is distinctive of the set or what is a superlative example of the set. Of course, there are no hard and fast rules here. Sometimes we do use "typical" and "epitome" interchangeably, or we add a "best" to "example" with a similar meaning in mind. What's important to notice, however, is that to be the best example or the most typical or the epitome of a set can itself be ambiguous between depicting what members of the set are generally like ("general typifying") and having in mind not what is generally true but rather making a value judgment about what the ideal member would look like and picking the closest example of that ("ideal typifying"). Which we use depends on our purposes.

For all their ambiguities, let's call these "typifying images." The typifying image minimally resembles the other members of the set. To have a typifying image of a set, we must have a set made of members that resemble one another in some significant way. Some sets have members that do not resemble one another much, if at all, beyond the trivial feature of being members of the same set. One could put typewriters, ghosts, and moon

---

7. Dictionary.com.

shots into the same set and one would be hard pressed to say how they resemble one another, whereas mules, donkeys, and horses would be easier to describe in terms of their resemblances. To have a typifying image, the set must be constructed of significantly resembling members. The more the members of the set resemble one another, the easier it is to say why these things belong to the set and the easier it is to find a typifying image. However, the resemblances need not be exactly the same in each member of the set.

There is obviously an overlap between dichotomous images and typifying images. As noted, sets can be made up of all sorts of wildly dissimilar things, so not all sets will have typifying imaging members. But typifying images do not merely represent the set. As we've seen, representation can be done with no resemblance at all (except perhaps the most general— being things, for example). To typify or epitomize, one has to resemble. In fact, one has to resemble *in the right way*. What is the right way? To some degree, that depends on the purposes one has. Consider "Joe is the image of a good (American) football player." (Notice the addition of "good" into the earlier example.) Is our purpose to pick out some set of general features of all football players? What would those be? It's not "big and burly" or "can run fast." Nor is it "good throwing arm" or "good on the catch." Wide receivers have different features than quarterbacks, and quarterbacks than centers. And all of them have different features than the defensive players. To typify a good football player *in general* may have little directly to do with the particular game of football: team player, ability to concentrate, etc. Perhaps better to say "Joe is the image of a good quarter back" or whatever one more specifically wants to pick out.

Consider the other example: "Mary is the image of a good CEO." (Again, note the addition of "good.") The category of "CEO" is in some ways narrower than that of football player, so perhaps it is tempting to respond that it is easier to say what would make a typifying member for CEOs than football players. Yet the problem doesn't go away. We could ask: "do you mean good CEO in terms of bringing in a huge profit, leading people well, knowing when to hire, when to fire, or speaks well to the board?" Without the "good," typifying the CEO might be easier (as it would be with football player). Any CEO would do, perhaps, so long as the CEO ran a corporation. Here the ambiguity between the ideal and the general comes to the fore. To be clear about a typifying image, we have to ask some detailed questions about what it is we want to capture; that is, what is our purpose in trying to typify or epitomize a set of entities?

IV

I turn now to a third and narrower but related sense of image. It is, perhaps, a philosopher's sense of image. Consider single-membered sets, sets consisting of a unique member. Take that member as an image of the members of the set. In that case, the singular set member images itself. Unlike with typifying images, where one thing epitomizes or typifies the other things in the set by resembling them, in this case, the thing that is the image just *is* (fully and completely) the thing in the set. Looked at in one way, such an image also epitomizes the members of the set, but in a narrowed down or even trivial sense of epitomize. In another sense, however, such an image truly epitomizes the members of the set because it simply is all the members of the set. It's not that one thing represents or copies the others in the set; the thing doing the imaging is the only thing in the set. "Resemblance," "copy," and "representation" are the wrong terms. "Presentation" is closer. The image presents itself or one could just as well say that the object presents itself. In short, the image just is the object and the object the image. In this case, the image truly does bring its object with it. I'll call this the "presentational image."

One final point about images. The typifying image appears to bridge dichotomous and presentational images. On the one hand, the typifying image resembles the other members of the set. On the other hand, the typifying image is a member of the set itself and thus presents at least one member of the set. Although not identical to the set, it is at least identical to one member of the set. It could be said to be a presentational image of the subset made up of the singular member that typifies the larger set.

V

To take up the topic of the image of God in humans, we need to reflect on what sort of image humans are. It is too quick and easy to simply replace the image language of the Scriptures with the philosophical language of essences. Further, I believe it is a mistake. To say humans have an essence—let's say (the capacity for) thought, emotional richness, will, and creativity—and that this is what the image of God is has been the approach of theologians since the early reflections on the biblical witness. Rationality is often the main term used to explain what the biblical writers meant when they unpacked the notion of the image of God in us. Here we confront some of the prejudices *against* images and *for* philosophical abstractions that rest in Plato's lap. Images mislead, he told us, whereas philosophy tells the truth. While I don't deny human essences (and in fact they are important for a variety of theological reasons) I do want to think more seriously about the image *qua* image. To say that we are made in the image of God is not the same as saying that certain universals are instantiated in us. To be *made* in the image of God is a making, not an instantiating from abstract universals to the concrete instances of those universals, even if the former (making) involves the latter (instantiating). Adam is made from dirt and God's breath into the image of God. It is too easy and quick, again, to treat the image language as mere metaphor and replace it with philosophical theory. What if we treat the language of image as literal, or at least as literally as we can?[8]

First, we have to acknowledge that in our being made in God's image there is no physical object (God is not physical) even though the resulting humans are themselves physical. In discussions of the image of God it is common to note that the image is *not* physical. What is typically meant is that our bodies do not have anything to do with the image of God that is in us. It is our spiritual or non-physical attributes that image God. But in walking that route we don't take the image language very seriously. Yet we make physical images of non-physical things with fair regularity. The flag is a physical image of freedom, for example. That is a representational image however, and it seems that what's going on with the image of God in humans is not merely representational (hence not merely socially created), but closer to copying.

But there are plenty of examples of physical images that copy, not merely represent, non-physical things. Consider the 1959 Cadillac. It is an image of American post-war self-congratulation and prowess, especially since Harley Earl (the designer) had American greatness in mind as he designed the largest tail fins for a car in history, right down to the bullet-shaped tail lights! One might note in this regard that many car designers of the 1950s used WW2 fighter planes as models for their work, which adds

---

8. I don't mean to imply that I think God literally made Adam out of the dust of the ground. But to say that God literally created an image of the divine self does not imply that every scriptural reference should be taken literally. God could very well have used (and I think probably did) an evolutionary scheme to make humans in the divine image. That can be literal without treating the text of Scripture as scientific description.

to the complexity of how physical and nonphysical symbols interact, but which also links the post-war self-congratulatory attitude to very physical images. One can begin with a non-physical notion (self-congratulation or prowess) and end up with a physical image of it.

Another sort of example of a physical image that copies a non-physical entity is a trademark for a corporation. In thinking about what a particular corporation is like (a corporation being not the people in it nor the business it engages in, but the non-physical, legal entity and perhaps its social features,) graphic artists try to capture in a physical image the "essence" of the corporation. We might think of Ronald MacDonald, for example, or the Nike "swoosh." (Here one might wonder why it is called a "swoosh" rather than a sloppy checkmark.) One finds something similar in book-cover images where a physical image captures the non-physical topic of a book. My book on how human noetic work makes the many ways the world is is called *Make/Believing the World(s)*. Its cover has a number of wooden building blocks with no letters, numbers, or colors on them and they are stacked in an order of some sort. That physical image captures the non-physical topic of the book quite well. Does it resemble the theme of the book? Yes. Does it copy it? Well, why not?

In like manner, humans in their very physical bodies may copy God's very non-physical being. Of course, there is lots of overlap between non-physical characteristics of the human person (thought, emotion, will, etc.) and the non-physical God. But in fact, for the most part our experience with the divine is embodied in people we know, the nature we experience, and, of course, the Jesus we love and worship. Nevertheless, it is not that difficult to grasp the plausibility of the idea that our very physical bodies copy the non-physical God. Our bodies act, think, create, and so on. The separation of these features of humans from the body is perhaps driven by the desire to turn the image language of Scripture into decorative metaphor.

But we need to say more, for the image of God into which we are made is arguably not a copy of God's properties—intellect, emotion, creativity, moral capacity, spirit, and so forth—but a copy of *God*. God of course has certain properties or capacities (God thinks, emotes, creates, is spirit, etc.). But in creating humans God is not making images of abstract entities but making images of the divine self. The properties God has are, of course, instantiated in the individual humans (as arguably they are in the divine persons), but the instantiation of properties is not the same thing as the making of the image or the image itself. The image—the made copy—is the *concrete person*, the *individual human*.

God's making us in the divine image seems to follow the same sort of pattern as we find in dichotomous imaging. First, there is something real and then a copy is made of it; object then image. But the image of God, as it is typically understood in theology, is a "shared" image. This is the place where it is tempting to ignore the actual language of Scripture, replacing the notion of image with the notion of essential properties that are shared by all humans *qua* human. But that is not what an image is.

Let's say two things accidentally resemble a third. Under those circumstances, we have resemblance but not copying. But in the making of X in the image of Y, one is not merely making a resemblance (although one is also doing that), one is copying. In the case of the accidental resemblance, there is no copy. Copied images seem to be singular, with each image an image of the object itself. The resemblance it has, let's say, to other copies is of course not totally accidental because each copy is a copy of the original, but neither is the resemblance among copies planned, or at least it need not be. Two copies of one object resemble each other not as copies of one another but as *copies of the original object*. A copied image is not a copy simply because it instantiates the same properties of the object. There is a causal history that is vital to its being a copy. *The image is a concrete, non-universal entity, a particular and historical uniqueness in the world*. The image of God that each of us is is an individual life with human properties instantiated in the particular space, time, culture, and peculiarities in which we find ourselves. Of course, one may worry whether such things as company logos (which must resemble each other in detail—being "exactly alike") is a sort of counterexample to what I've just said. I don't believe it. Although logos are, of course, more similar to one another in general than humans are, they are still located in space and time in a way that arguably makes them unique. So Ronald MacDonald is an image of MacDonald's, but each instance of the Ronald MacDonald image is somewhat unique.

A problem may arise here. If we start with the image as a real entity and have that as the primary sort of thing each of us is (with each individual copy of God standing on its own, so to speak) and then understand the shared properties as secondary (with our commonality not being the main feature of humans), don't we end up with the image of God as shaky ground for sin and salvation? That conclusion is too hasty. That we are unique copies of God individually does not entail that there is nothing in common among us. It only places the commonalities in the right perspective.

In other words, what I've suggested does not deny that insofar as each of us is made in God's image we each resemble one another or that we instantiate essential properties. But *it is the copying that makes us in the image of God* and not the resembling or instantiating *per se*. Consider an analogy. All copy-images, say, of Mount Denali share some set of common properties in virtue of which they are images of Denali, just as all copy-images of God share something in common in virtue of which they are images of God. Now it is primarily because they are copies of Denali that they resemble Denali, they are not copy-images of Denali just because they resemble one another. No resemblance the images have to one another is enough to make them copies of Denali. They could resemble one another and be copies of each other without being copies of Denali. So it is with humans. We could all resemble one another, or we could all be instantiations of certain properties *without being copy-images of God*. In fact, that is often what secular philosophies from the Enlightenment on have said. No need for God, just a need for some sort of Platonic essences in the universe that all humans happen to share and that is enough to ground, for example, ethical treatment.

Be that as it may, if we want to emphasize the uniqueness of the image of God that each of us is—that is, if we want to emphasize the fact that we are *made* images of God—we'll need to say more of how the instantiation of a property is a unique instantiation. The notion of essences and instantiation is a large and complicated topic. There are a variety of ways in which the term "essence" is used. We are working here with kind-essences. When we think of kind-essences, we typically think of necessary properties. To be a member of a kind (here I'm talking about natural kinds rather than artifactual kinds—dogs and stars rather than cogs and cars) is to have certain properties without which one wouldn't be in the kind. Whatever the properties are that make humans human, we all have them. Often, and for the most part traditionally, essences or necessary properties are thought of along realist lines. By "realist" I mean that for the vast majority of natural things in the world, they are what they are independent of human noetic contributions. So cows have bovine essential properties independent of what any human person wishes about, believes about, or otherwise thinks about cows. Kinds (natural ones, at any rate) are found or discovered, not made, by humans.

Image, Incarnation, and Expansivism

However, one need not be a strict realist about properties in order for kinds to be rooted in a reality independent of human noetic work. In fact, taking a more relaxed (partly irrealistic) approach to essences allows for more diversity among the individual (copied) images as I described them above. When talking about the essence of being human (the supposed image of God) it is common to take that essence realistically so that the image of God in you is the same as the image of God in me. Rationality, emotional richness, volition, etc., all turn up in each of us as realist essential properties. But perhaps the set of properties shared among humans need not be instantiations of the same abstract essence, *except in a fairly limited way*. Perhaps, instead, we each receive what I'll call a "Wittgensteinian family resemblance" set of properties.

The standard Wittgensteinian picture (as many seem to conceive of it), claims that if A, B, C, D, and E resemble one another, A is like B, B like C, and so forth, but A may not resemble E. That is, A may share no (resembling) properties with E. Hence, one game is like another and that one like another and so forth, but the last game may not share anything in common with the first game, except being called a game. I propose a different view. By "Wittgensteinian family resemblances" I intend the following. Although A and E may be quite dissimilar, A and E still resemble each other because they have the same *thin essence*.

Here we'll need some explanation of thin vs. thick essences and concepts. Let's say a thin concept is the basic idea of something and thick concepts flesh out the basic idea of that thing. Thick concepts can go in quite different directions from one another. In other words, concepts are fluid rather than crystalline. Fluid concepts are malleable, crystalline concepts are not. As an example of how this all might work, consider two philosophers who agree on the following thin concept: the mind is the thing that thinks. But they might disagree on how to thicken up the thin concept. One takes the thin concept in the direction of the thicker concept of dualism (the mind is the thing that thinks, but does so without need of a brain) and the other philosopher takes the thin concept in the direction of the thick concept of materialism (the mind *just is* the brain). Having the idea of thin vs. thick concepts in front of us, we can say that a thin essence picks out what a thing is via thin concepts and a thick essence picks out what a thing is via thick concepts. One can also speak of thin properties (related to the thin concepts of those properties) and thick properties (related to the thick concepts of those properties). In addition, thin concepts, properties, and essences will hold in all conceptual schemes, thick concepts only in some conceptual schemes.

A thin essence is made up of thin properties. Thin properties are more or less stripped down properties, properties that depend on thin concepts. Such a concept will be filled out in the world by one's conceptual scheme, noetic framework, and historical situation. How one thinks about the concept "mind" will, of course, be situated in one's place in history which in turn will be influenced by one's noetic commitments (including cultural understandings) and the particular conceptual scheme one has developed. Conceptual schemes include the richer, more filled out accounts of the thin concepts. One does not typically consider only the thin properties and their related essences or concepts of a thing unless one is considering the question: how are all these things united? One can and should ask that question, of course, and when it is asked, one turns to the barest account of the essence to place things into a resemblance set. So a set of entities is in the same resemblance set when considered on the thin level. The thin properties a thing has could hold across all conceptual schemes, noetic frameworks, and historical situations and thus provide for essences across schemes, frameworks, and situations.

The thick properties, however, those that are embedded in the conceptual schemes, noetic frameworks, and historical situations, provide for various levels of uniqueness. In many instances, two things could resemble each other a great deal and in other cases not so much. Here is where Wittgensteinian resemblances enter the picture. Two members of the set at opposite ends of the resemblance continuum that ground a resemblance set would still (necessarily) have enough in common so that one could recognize them as members of the same set. The thin essences unite a set of objects but those thin essences are sometimes hard to uncover, for one has to dig down through various thickened up accounts of the thin essences to find the thin. Here we need to consider typifying images briefly. One of the reasons for limiting Wittgensteinian resemblances the way I do is that if A and E (on opposite ends of the continuum) don't resemble each other at all, then it's hard to see how one could have a typifying member of the set, whether general or ideal.

Let's consider an example from the list of supposed essential properties typically used by theologians. Being rational on the thin level, let's say, is the property of assessing claims for truth and acting on those claims. Now two philosophers could thicken up that property in quite different ways via alternative conceptual schemes (or alternative noetic frameworks). Looking at the philosophical literature on rationality, one could have one's pick about how to thicken up the property. Any two of those ways of thickening up the thin notion of rationality may be contradictory to one another. Typically that is reason to reject at least one of them. However, if a claim is true only within a conceptual scheme, noetic framework, or historical circumstance, then what is true is relative to conceptual schemes, noetic frameworks, or historical circumstances and the claims are not contradictory unless removed, *per impossible*, from their situations.[9] Two people living their lives according to rationality, hence, might be living in two substantially different ways. One's rationality might not agree with another's at all, in fact. This (irrealist) way of considering essences allows for necessary properties at the thin level, but not at the thicker level. What is true at a thick level within a situation depends not on the "real" way the world is but on a variety of features deriving from the conceptual scheme, noetic framework, or historical circumstance. But still, at the thin level, it will turn out true in every situation that humans have certain thin essential properties.

By way of analogy, when Nelson Goodman is considering realism in painting, he makes the following observations. He describes two pictures, one realistic (that is, what we Westerners typically take to be realist, one that "looks like" nature, whose perspective is "ordinary" and whose colors are "normal") and one in reverse perspective and whose colors are replaced by the normal colors's complements. He then says this:

> The two pictures . . . are equally correct, equally faithful to what they represent, provide the same and hence equally true information; yet they are not equally realistic or literal. For a picture to be faithful is simply for the object represented to have the properties that the picture in effect ascribes to it. But such fidelity or correctness or truth is not a sufficient condition for literalism or realism. The alert absolutist will argue that for the second picture but not the first we need a key. [In response,] . . . the difference is that for the first the key is ready at hand. . . . Just here, I think, lies the touchstone of realism [in the arts]: not in quantity of information but in how easily it issues. And this depends upon how stereotyped the mode of representation is, upon how commonplace the labels and their uses have become.[10]

9. See my *Make/Believing the World(s)* for further details on how this account might go.

10. Goodman, *Languages of Art*, 36.

The analogy is this.: Just as what counts as a realistic painting depends not merely on content but on how easily the representation unmasks itself—how easily it issues from the painting—so the truth about human persons depends not merely on description but on how easily the truth unmasks itself from the historical circumstances. One can find, in short, the thin essential properties underneath the layers of thickened up descriptions and layers of historically rooted lives. So there is a real basis (a basis not relying on our histories, conceptual schemes, and noetic frameworks) that ties us all together and yet each of us is unique in that we copy God in the particular, historically situated way that we do. Each of Goodman's pictures stands in a copy (he says representational) relationship with what they copy but they are quite different and distinct portrayals of their object. Although quite different, they are equally real presentations of their objects even though one might be less familiar.

Thus while each person shares the same thin properties, how those properties are thickened up depends on historically rooted conceptual-schematic features. Thus, what being rational looks like for one person may be quite different from what it looks like for another. So instead of Wittgensteinian resemblances varying so much between A and E because A and E fail to have any properties in common, A and E can *appear* to have little in common because the thickened up versions of the properties are so disparate. All of this is consistent with the idea that God makes us in the divine image as copies of God. God is the object and each of us, in our historical, conceptually nuanced context, develops into the thickened up instantiation of the thin properties. Because we are made as images of God, the thin properties are always thickened up by the historical circumstance and its related (set of) conceptual schemes and noetic frameworks.

The result of all this is that humans copy God, and hence resemble God, via historically conditioned properties that are copied from God in rather unique ways. Humans also resemble (but do not copy) each other at the thin level.[11] Copying involves God being present to the causal chain of each human's development whereas resemblance does not. Some of the differences in resemblance (even radical ones) can be explained via the Wittgensteinian resemblance properties being different from one another in quite significant ways at the thick level and yet similar enough at the thin

---

11. Of course, there is a sort of copying going on with our genetically related children and ourselves. However, even there the copying seems to lack the *intentional* control over what the children are like.

level to count individuals as members of the same resemblance set. This resemblance, thus, is not accidental.

Returning now more fully to the typifying image, we might ask for a typifying example of humanity in a theological context. Our first inclination might be to say that anyone of us might be as good as any other to typify humanity. Let's say that what it is to be human is to be made in the image of God. Each and every human is made thus. If we want to talk about thin properties that are essential to humans, we might say that to be human is to be capable (in principle) of rationality, emotions, creativity, free choices, or spirituality.[12] Once again, any one of us would fit the bill as typical.

But what of the other sense of typifying image—the ideal typifying image? Here we run into some substantial difficulties, for if we are in the set "human" because we resemble one another, we resemble one another in Wittgensteinian resemblances rooted in thin essential properties, at least according to my account. That is, we run into the problem that humans are so varied and indeed unique that it is hard to point to any singular set of features by which one human can be suggested as an ideal. Since the ideal typifying image requires us to make certain value judgments, the vast differences among us might incline us to narrow the field. We might want to ask which aspects of humanity we desire to typify. Is it courage, creativity, rationality with emotional sensitivity or something else? We might propose, for example, the heroic among us, or the great inventors, leaders, or other "important" figures. But if we try to pick out the ideal *human*, we are probably going to run into challenges of all sorts. There is a theological answer, however. Jesus might be the only human who fits the ideal account for not only has he all the properties at the thin level that go into making up the human person but he also lacks a property that keeps the rest of us from being ideal, viz., sin. Whereas many other superlative human persons are superlative in having various of the thin properties thickened up in

---

12. Here it is important to note that all humans, even those who are extremely mentally challenged and have lived, let's say, in a permanent vegetative state since birth are made in the image of God. Hence the importance when putting the image of God into philosophical terms to speak of "capacities in principle." It is also theologically (and morally) important to consider that Jesus holds up children as models of spirituality. "Let the children come to me, for to such belong the kingdom of heaven." He also indicates that the least will be the greatest and it is not difficult to infer that the most mentally challenged human will be, in fact, the greatest in the kingdom of heaven. As such, we may be honoring saints in serving those among us who are the least capable now of serving anyone.

interesting and powerful ways, no one but Jesus can claim to be superlative in being without sin (by nature).[13]

In addition, the fact that Jesus is without sin also implies that he is physically, psychologically, and emotionally whole and complete. While he is the unique person he is, he would also not suffer from the challenges and problems the rest of us have in terms of dealing with the stresses of life. I'm not saying he would not feel stress or anguish, etc., but only that he would be capable of handling it well and appropriately. In this sense he would be a superlative human as well.

Finally, the presentational image appears to be the sort of image that Christ is of God insofar as Jesus is divine. Since he is God, he doesn't copy God, at least in the sense that we find him described in Colossians 1:15–20. So the image that Jesus is of God is a presentational image. Equally truly, I am the presentational image of myself. Since I am a member of the single-membered set made up solely of myself, I presentationally image myself, as do you yourself, and your neighbor herself and so on.

VI

I want to weave these various themes together with some reflections on sin and salvation. Jesus is the presentational image of God, the unique member of the set "divine-human persons." That makes him unique, not only among humans, but among all the things in the universe. It would be a mistake, however, to think that that is all there is to Jesus' uniqueness, viz., that he has a divine history. He also has a human history that is unique. He was born of Mary, taught carpentry by Joseph, walked along the road between Jerusalem and Bethany on a certain day in the year 27 and so forth. We "regular" humans are unique in that same way. We are born of the particular parents we are, raised in the neighborhoods we are, etc. In that way, each of us is the presentational image of ourselves.

Jesus' unique history as a divine person, however, includes becoming human and staying human. That is, the second person of the Trinity is forever the divine-human. When the New Testament speaks of Jesus as the image of God (see Col 1:15–20; 2 Cor 4:4 and the related John 14:9; Heb 1:1–4; Eph 4:17–24; Rom 8:3; and Phil 2:7–8—I'll return to these in the last chapter in more detail), it speaks of us seeing God (in the divine self) when

---

13. Here one might suggest the Roman Catholic version of Mary. She, however, is sinless by grace, not nature. In fact, we can all become sinless by grace.

we see Jesus the human. The two are not separated, as Chalcedon recognizes when it says Jesus has two natures and two wills but is one person. To see Jesus the human is the see Jesus the divine creator of the universe.

What has that to do with our being made in the image of God? Just this. If Jesus is truly human, then he too is made in God's image. That is, Jesus is as much the dichotomous image of God as we are. That explains, if my earlier description is right, why Jesus is unique as a human. He is a unique copy of God, as is each of us. Yet there is something else about Jesus that is unique. When a "regular" human is made, she is made from scratch as a copy of God. But Jesus pre-exists his human incarnation and thus, in a sense, *he copies humans* when he is made the incarnate God. Whereas we all resemble one another because we copy God, Jesus resembles us because he copies us.

But Jesus copies us without sin. Sin, of course, is adventitious to humans. It is not a necessary property. When God incarnates as a human, he does not copy us in that respect. To put it as the Orthodox would, the image of God is separate from the likeness of God in the creation of humanity. The image of God is our reason, will, emotional richness, and creativity. But the likeness of God is our capacity for virtue, our capacity to be fully like God *in the human way*. Jesus becomes like God *in the human way* in his incarnation. We see God in Jesus because he has grown into the sort of reliance on God that is needful for true sanctification (true deification, as the Orthodox would say). He has by nature what we can have by grace. By nature, he never was sinful. He chose, in his earthly life, to shape his earthly being after God's will, not his own human will. That makes him the full image of God as a human. So not only is he God by nature, but he is the ideal typifying image of God as well, a human without sin, totally reliant on the will of God. His human will is amalgamated to God's will and he thus lives out the life of God on earth.

So Jesus is the presentational image of God (God in the divine self), the ideal typifying image of a human (in his sinless humanity), and the dichotomous image of God in his being made the unique human he is, a copy of God. Salvation is provided by God in Jesus because of the way these three images work together. Because Jesus is a copy of God as we are, his presence among us is related to us via both his uniqueness from us and his commonality with us. He is, via the thin properties that we all share, and in virtue of which we more or less resemble each other, the savior for all humanity. But he copies us as well in his uniqueness, his historicity, his being thickened up according to a conceptual scheme or noetic structure that places him very much among the finite and contingent. His uniqueness is, in short, just as much a part of the image of God as is the fact that he shares the properties necessary for his being a human. But it is because he is the unique, particular example of the ideal human that we can learn to become like God as well (on the Orthodox view). He chose to be like God and hence imaged God in the full way a human ought to and not merely in his rationality, emotional richness, or creativity. He lived the life of sinlessness and thereby is the example of how it can be done.

Thus we have the image of God, as much unique as it is shared. The implications of our uniqueness are not limited to the evolution of our individual ways of being in the world, but extend to the development of the wide variety of cultures and expressions of the celebration of the life God gives us. And it also influences how we should understand the nature of (original) sin and the nature of our salvation. We come to God both corporately and individually. As I noted in chapter 1, when the rich young man asks Jesus what he must do to be saved, Jesus asks him if he'd followed the law. He had! Then the Lord says he lacks one more thing. He is to sell all his possessions and to follow Jesus. That is a very different approach to the particulars of salvation than he tells Nicodemus, the woman at the well, and Martha. Each of us comes to salvation in unique circumstances with our unique personalities, but also with the knowledge that we are all related to Jesus our brother and it is that relatedness that means Jesus' singular life, death, and resurrection can save us.

The uniqueness of our circumstances points to the importance of our understanding sin not as a sort of deposit placed in or on us at birth, but as a developmental feature of our being humans shaped by our own choices. The notion of original sin is protean in meaning but standardly claims that we are born with a propensity to turn away from God toward unrighteousness, a propensity we all follow. But the propensity is strong enough that the church fretted over whether unbaptized children entered heaven. Original sin, more or less like the essential characteristics that make one human, is just present in everyone from birth (or conception) onward. Original sin is, so to speak, generic sin—the same in all of us. My point about our uniquenesses and sin is just this: it's not merely generic sin I need to be saved from, it is *my* sin—sin that I own, that I live in and into. Because sin is both generic and unique to me, salvation must be generic and unique to me. We need both. The generic, one-size-fits-all notion of salvation does not do justice to my one-of-a-kind, historically rooted sin. The image of God in us needs to explain *both*. So we should celebrate our commonalities—they bind us together in our lives—but we should equally celebrate our uniqueness and our diversity, for that is, indeed, the way the image of God is.

But if the image of God is diverse, and hence sin is diverse, shouldn't salvation be diverse? Not if one is an access exclusivist. It is to that topic that I turn in the next chapter.

Chapter 3

Existentially Problematic Salvific Exclusivism

Recall that the holder of Christian salvific exclusivism believes that there is only one true description of salvific reality and that no other description, save the Christian one, is true. That is the metaphysical realist component from chapter 1. Further, the holder of Christian salvific exclusivism (CSE) believes that entering into a proper relationship with God through Jesus Christ is necessary and sufficient to be saved. This is the ontologically monist component. I want to keep these two components separate from the third, viz., how we humans access God through Jesus—the access component. Jesus is the path to salvation in God, but for the holder of CSE there is a particular or unique human means of accessing that path. Of course, for many exclusivists, it may be true that one's ontological view determines the nature of human access to salvation. Nevertheless, I will treat the access component as practically separate.

According to CSE, in order to be saved one must be in the appropriate relationship with God through Jesus Christ via the power of the Holy Spirit. This raises a very important question. Which of the many options on the table is the appropriate means of accessing a proper relationship with Jesus Christ? How does one achieve the appropriate relationship? What activities does one need to engage in? Assuming that the fused model of CSE is correct, are those activities external activities (participating in Mass or child

Image, Incarnation, and Expansivism

baptism, etc.) or internal activities (a life of serious prayer or a simple faith in the work Christ did)? And if it is faith that supports the appropriate relationship, what is one's faith to be in? Is it enough, for example, to believe that Jesus died on the cross in your place *sans* commitment to his being the Christ or, indeed, God? What about all those Arian Christians, both past and present? Or suppose you accept that Jesus is God but that he didn't *really* die on the cross since you think God can't die? As I said, there are many questions to raise here.

In order to focus on the access questions I will leave the ontology question unanswered in this chapter. So far as ontology goes, it seems fairly clear that in Christianity it is the incarnate life, death, and resurrection of Jesus Christ that provides the structure supporting any salvation of a human person. So I will raise no quibble at this juncture with the ontological claim that Jesus' work in his earthly life, suffering, death, and resurrection provide the necessary salvific ontological base. But those theological and ontological features do not themselves tell us how to go about accessing the salvific work of God. I concentrate thus on the varied means by which Christians have thought to access the ontological framework of salvation. I will take up two challenges. The first is presented in section I. It is unsuccessful but provides a backdrop to a more successful second challenge, which is presented in section II.

I

Before I get to the first, if unsuccessful argument, consider the deep background of the issue of salvific exclusivism. There is a general and commonly made observation about metaphysical realism (taken as a whole and not simply as applied to Christianity). Metaphysical realism appears to be undermined by the presence of many intractable conflicts about ontological (and other) matters. Because of these intractable issues, we find many philosophers who simply move to radical versions of antirealism for it seems the best explanation for the many varied and often equally well-evidenced ontological positions. *I do not, in fact, think such arguments work.* But one can reject the logic of an argument and recognize the existential or psychological force that it has. With that observation in view, I turn to the first challenge to CSE.

An argument similar to the one just noted can be proposed against CSE. According to the CSE Christian, there is only one true account of the universe and the God who created it. Presumably, this description includes the true account of the necessary and sufficient relationship to Jesus Christ for the provision of salvation. Attached to those two views, as I've been discussing, is the view that there is but one means by which the salvific ontology of Christianity can be accessed.[1] That said, one challenge to CSE is what appears to be an embarrassment of riches in regard to the theological understandings of exactly what brings one into an appropriate relationship to Jesus. This embarrassment of riches seems, in fact, simply to undermine the claim of metaphysical realism that attends CSE. In short, the metaphysical realist component of CSE seems undermined by the plain empirical fact that among Christians exists a rich and contradictory set of accounts of how to access the salvific ontology. Indeed, both across the ages and across the current denominational spread there seems to be little agreement about what brings one into the appropriate relationship with Jesus Christ. Even further, within any given church one might find many fused versions of exclusive access to salvation. Which of the many descriptions of the access to salvation is the one and only correct one?

As noted above, I don't think the general argument against metaphysical realism works. So it should be little surprise that I don't think the particular application of the argument in the context of Christian exclusivism works either. So why introduce it? Basically, it serves as a good backdrop to the second challenge, viz., that the many conflicting accounts of salvific access create, in the context of realist Christianity, a substantial *existential* problem for the Christian salvific exclusivist. So let's begin by raising the questions, why are there so many conflicting accounts of salvific access and which of those accounts is the correct one?

One might suggest that this issue is merely epistemological. That is, one might suggest that while there are many understandings of the salvific access, only one of them is true. Our inability to agree on which one is true is due mainly to our epistemic short comings, either because of finitude or sin. Nevertheless, one should find the correct path, for it, and only it, is the salvific road that one must follow.

Now while this might be enough to respond to the challenge in principle, I suggest that it is not enough in practice. It surely would leave many Christians out of heaven—perhaps too many. Consider the following. In the high-church traditions (Roman Catholic, Orthodox, and Anglican) it

---

1. Or if more than one, that fact is due to contingent circumstances, such as the gospel not being communicated or not communicated well.

is possible to find many who participate in Eucharist regularly but whose faith in God or Jesus is, from one point of view, quite limited. They have been raised to think, let's say, that participating in the Eucharist is itself enough to bring them into a salvific relationship with Jesus. This is, of course, a very thin theology as well as a poor understanding of what these various branches of Christianity teach. It is, nevertheless, what many would be found believing. Note that it is not simply sophisticated theological understandings that come into play in terms of the question of salvific access, but the beliefs or attitudes of every single Christian, no matter how atypical, incorrect, or unorthodox her theology may be. After all, the vast majority of Christians believe that they are following a path that will lead them, finally, into God's presence.

In contrast to the high-church Christians just described, in many (lower church) evangelical Protestant churches, one will find an emphasis on faith and faith alone as the mainspring bringing one to a proper relationship with Jesus. This too is often poorly understood, often far removed from Luther's original emphasis on faith alone. Many evangelicals treat faith as if it were an entirely personal relationship between an individual and Jesus that has little to do with anything beside a very personal piety and getting into heaven. Indeed, one way to think of these two salvific paths (the low-church evangelical view and Luther's) is to contrast Luther's criticism of "theologies of glory" and his own development of a theology of the cross. Luther's theology of the cross was no "easy-believism," as my Bible-college evangelism instructor might have referred to the way some think of faith.

Now of these two understandings of how to obtain a proper relationship with Jesus—the highchurch and the evangelical lowchurch—at best only one can be accurate from a CSE point of view. If we suppose one of these Christian understandings is the right one, then many Christians are simply not going to make it into the kingdom. But the situation is only made worse when one thinks of all the varieties of human personality, our historical upbringings, and our existential situations. Given all this variety of human experience, and the notion of fused access to the salvation of Christ, there will be many human ways of accessing the grace of God. Which of those ways is, in fact, the correct way?

A hardliner on CSE might just say, "wide is the gate and broad is the road that leads to destruction, and many enter through it. But small is the gate and narrow the road that leads to life, and only a few find it." Exegetical questions about that passage aside, perhaps the epistemological approach to the issue still stands. Maybe not only very few get into the kingdom but perhaps even very few Christians. Perhaps the hardliner on CSE is right and we need to look very diligently at Scripture alongside the histories of theology and the church to decide which path is the correct one. Perhaps in the end the number of people who are genuinely saved is quite small, or at least, quite a bit smaller than we might think (or hope) at first glance. But while the epistemological situation in which we find ourselves can be challenging enough, there is a deeper problem here.

II

So I think there is a related challenge that has more bite. Here the issue isn't just that we might be limited in our epistemic abilities to decide among the many paths. Rather, the issue is stronger in that no matter what proposal one puts forth, the evidence is never enough to decide. The theologies of salvific access are thick and messy and each one seems underdetermined by the evidence. Or, put another way, the evidence supports too many views.

Which of the two accounts—the high church and low church—gets at how one ought to go about developing the right, that is, the salvific, relationship with God through Jesus? These two stories are dual tips of a very large iceberg. It certainly is not clear from Scripture that there is just one proper path to salvation in terms of answering the host of access questions I've listed. Even the Gospel accounts of Jesus don't help us out. If anything, they leave us scratching our heads. The point is not just that there are many different results one might get from a survey of the epistemological options and since only one of them is right we just need to look hard to find the proper course. Rather, the issue is that no matter how hard one looks, the evidence that is supposed to help you decide is never strong enough to properly ground one's decision over against others one could make. The sort of appeal William Craig makes to a number of biblical references can surely be countered by many other such appeals.[2] Like so many theological questions, exegesis alone won't answer some of the most basic issues.

But perhaps the holder of CSE might respond simply by digging in his heels. That is, perhaps he will simply refuse to accept the observation about the under-determination of the evidence for how one should develop the proper salvific relationship. He'll pick his view and stick with it, pointing out as much evidence as he can while explaining away as much

2. Craig, "No Other Name."

counter-evidence as he can. Although the critic certainly can dig in his epistemological heels, it seems that too many thoughtful people have come to intellectual (and sometimes not so intellectual) blows over which is the right path. So I believe the problem shifts from merely being epistemological to being metaphysical or theological.

It is important to note that I am not simply arguing from the intractable nature of the various theological or ontological conflicts to some sort of pluralism. I don't believe that sort of argument works. Rather, the problem is theological, and internally so, because of other things taught in the Christian faith. To make this clear, the basic question I want to raise at this juncture is: what kind of God would provide for the possibility of salvation for human persons but then make it so difficult to discover how to access it? While I think it is abundantly clear that God in Christ is the ontological basis for salvation and that Jesus is the proper means of accessing God's salvation, it is not clear which of the many conflicting access stories in the New Testament one should follow.

One way of looking at the problem is to take it as an application of the hiddenness-of-God challenge, but one deeply ingrained within the Christian faith itself. God hides not just in general but even within the multiple approaches of the Christian faith. Here, once again, the critic can remain committed to the view that there is nothing going on except the challenge of our epistemological situation. The metaphysically realist aspect of CSE allows for a kind of skepticism about whether one has actually gotten the truth. There is a single "way things are" and that is that. Whether anyone has actually found the right path is irrelevant to the logic or truth of CSE. We can call such a view "salvific skepticism" and its adherents "salvific skeptics." Note that the salvific skeptic is not saying that no one has gotten the truth or gained knowledge or even gained rational belief. The point really is a kind of separation of the epistemology of the situation from the ontology. What is real is real, whether anyone accesses it or not.

The argument now takes a different direction. To follow that turn in the argumentative road, it is helpful to remind ourselves that at the very least, Christianity is a life-ordering story. Whether Roman Catholic, Orthodox or Protestant, conservative or liberal, charismatic or emergent, Christianity is a central framework around which people organize their lives. Insofar as people take their eternal salvation (in whatever guise they might understand that) seriously, Christianity involves a type of surety about one's beliefs or knowledge. While not everyone has such surety, it

Existentially Problematic Salvific Exclusivism

is nevertheless an important aspect of the relationship between God and those people who try to access salvation. If a person doesn't have some sort of psychological certitude about having properly accessed the salvific ontology, she more than likely longs to have such salvific certitude. Salvation is a very important notion in Christianity—one might say the most important notion. What, after all, is more central to the Christian religion than God's relationship to human sinners? Salvation and one's personal, existential awareness of it seems absolutely central to the very nature of the Christian tradition. Such a relationship cannot be reduced to believing the right propositions about oneself or God. I do not mean to say, of course, that one lacking such salvific certitude is not among the redeemed. To say that salvific certitude is central to the Christian tradition is only to note its frequent presence among Christians and, where it is lacking, a desire for its presence. The existential nature of Christianity should not be overlooked merely because we are taking an analytic approach to the philosophical or theological questions.

Here we enter into the pastorally philosophical realm most directly. I want to emphasize again that my goal is not to work merely on a theoretical problem but a lived problem, a problem that faces many Christians in their existential circumstances. By calling attention to the existential or spiritual issue I hope to show that the best recourse is better teaching in our churches so that the existential issues are lifted. That is why the fact that some groups of Christians (fundamentalists and/or evangelicals were my examples, but there could be others as well) function *as if* CSE were true is relevant, even if no one officially teaches CSE.

Of course, to analyze the various aspects of the existential nature of Christian ways of being in the world is a tall order. To take up the turn in the argument more specifically, perhaps it will suffice to distinguish between, on the one hand, (rationally) believing or knowing certain propositions and, on the other, the psychological range of commitments and attitudes that can attach not only to the truth of the propositions but the reality behind them. That is, let's think not merely of propositional attitudes but attitudes of other sorts, including emotional attachments toward things and persons—the entities behind, so to speak, the propositions. These will include hope, love, psychological certitude (and a whole range of less strong feelings of surety), and so forth.

Consider the following as a brief nonreligious illustration in order to clarify just one aspect of these "extra epistemological" features of any epistemological situation. Suppose my wife calls and asks if I locked the car when I left it in the office parking lot today. She wants to make sure, let's say, that some important papers she put in the car are safe. So I tell her I did lock the car. She might well say, "Do you know you did?" I might reply that I do know, explicitly expressing a knowledge claim. Now that she has raised the issue about my knowledge, I will also believe that I know that I locked the car. Such a belief comes to the surface of my consciousness, becoming not merely dispositional but occurrent. Let's call this the "straight" epistemology of the situation.

But there are also extra-epistemological aspects surrounding claims to knowledge or rational belief. We can, for example, talk about how committed I am to the belief that I know and, in fact, how committed I am to the belief in question itself (viz., that I locked the car). Typically, knowledge of the sort that I locked the car is not very important to me. Indeed, I wouldn't typically say that I'm very committed to individual bits of knowledge of that sort at all. Should I discover that I didn't actually know, it would not have much effect on me. Often when I believe I know that I locked the car (or similar beliefs), I don't check out the truth of my belief. But at the time my wife calls, perhaps my commitment to the belief that I know needs to be a little higher. In fact, perhaps it's worth checking to see if I did, in fact, lock the car. That I subsequently go to check my knowledge claim does not entail that I don't know that the car is locked. Neither does the fact that I typically wouldn't check entail that I do, in fact, know. One's knowledge and the level of one's commitment to having that knowledge are not the same thing. Whatever knowledge is, the point here is simply that one can have other attitudes that surround instances of knowing. These are not always propositional attitudes either. My attitude of care for my wife plays in here, as I will be motivated to check my claim to knowledge not out of some strange philosophical curiosity but out of love for my wife. Whatever such attitudes toward my wife might be, my deciding to check whether I locked the car may strengthen my knowledge that I locked the car. Or it may simply strengthen my belief that I know. Or it may strengthen other attitudes surrounding the knowledge claim or my emotional connection to the things or people involved. Alternatively, should I find the car unlocked, checking my knowledge claim would end up totally undermining it along with the belief that I know that I locked the car.

Here it is helpful to introduce contextualism from contemporary analytic theory of knowledge. The term "knows" may be context-sensitive.

Matthew McGrath writes: "'Knows' varies in its sense across contexts of speech in such a way that 'S knows P' can have one sense in one context of use and another in another context."³ Here's a typical example to illustrate, taken from Keith DeRose.

> *Bank Case A.* My wife and I are driving home on a Friday afternoon. We plan to stop at the bank on the way home to deposit our paychecks. But as we drive past the bank, we notice that the lines inside are very long, as they often are on Friday afternoons. Although we generally like to deposit our paychecks as soon as possible, it is not especially important in this case that they be deposited right away, so I suggest that we drive straight home and deposit our paychecks on Saturday morning. My wife says, "Maybe the bank won't be open tomorrow. Lots of banks are closed on Saturdays." I reply, "No, I know it'll be open. I was just there two weeks ago on Saturday. It's open until noon."

> *Bank Case B.* [the same as Case A but . . .] in this case, we have just written a very large and important check. If our paychecks are not deposited into our checking account before Monday morning, the important check we wrote will bounce, leaving us in a *very* bad situation. And, of course, the bank is not open on Sunday. My wife reminds me of these facts. She then says, "Banks do change their hours. Do you know the bank will be open tomorrow?" Remaining as confident as I was before that the bank will be open then, still, I reply, "Well, no. I'd better go in and make sure."⁴

It is important to note that in this sort of example, one remains just as confident of one's belief, but it seems that what it means for one to know depends on the context. One's evidence, which standards one meets, how strong one's justification is, etc., all remain the same. So either one fails to speak the truth that one knows in the first case or one fails to speak the truth in the second case. Or the contextualist alternative is right: "know" means different things in different contexts.

What's interesting is that it is *the encroachment of the pragmatic* that shifts the context. When it comes to Christian beliefs, the relationship among beliefs, knowledge, and the host of other commitments and attitudes is, if anything, far more complicated than the example just provided. After all, what is at stake isn't just some important papers or even the very

3. McGrath "Contextualism," 108.
4. DeRose, "Contextualism and Knowledge," 108.

important relationship with my wife or the very bad situation one might be in were a check to bounce. It is, in the case we are discussing, the salvation of one's very being and the relationship with one's creator, which enfolds all other things of importance.

Here let me introduce a real-life problem I encountered recently in one of my classes. I teach at an evangelical university. We have a good number of very bright students, including some in our philosophy major. In a class on feminist thought that I teach, we read a book on the history of evangelical feminism. One student asked something close to the following question: "How are we to interpret any passage of Scripture and know we've got it right if we cannot interpret the few passages on the role of women in the church or the family?" His look was not one of mere intellectual curiosity. He looked more as if he was hanging over the abyss and the structures of interpretation he had learned in his church had fallen out from underneath him. Did he know anything that he had been taught at home and in church about his own salvation? What he thought he knew he now wondered deeply about. The context had shifted as he learned about the breadth and difficulty of interpreting the Scriptures. "Know" was taking on a new sense.

With these observations as background, note that salvific skepticism (as attached to CSE) runs the risk of overlooking, or even denying, the very existential nature of the problem I've been discussing. I suggest that, in fact, salvific skepticism, while appearing to be simply a philosophical retreat, actually involves a deep existential problem, viz., *that one can never have good existential grounds to be assured of one's salvation*. What one needs to know and perhaps thought one knew, slips away. The pragmatic situation becomes very pressing since one's very salvation relies on finding the proper understanding of how to obtain the appropriate relationship with Jesus. While the retreat to the epistemic safety of salvific skepticism defends the possibility of CSE, it does so only at the price of undermining one's existential life within the core of the gospel story, viz., the love of God for human persons and the whole of the created order, along with the divine desire to provide salvation for the much beloved humans and their created environment. In choosing salvific skepticism (and thus radically separating epistemic concerns from ontological issues) it appears that a rather startling commitment to a philosophical protectionism (wherein one holds onto a particular philosophical thesis—realism linked to single ontology and narrow access Christianity) is chosen over against one's spiritual and emotional connection to God's love. The situation seems parallel to a parent who truly loves her child. The child, however, will die without access to a particular medical treatment. Yet the parent gives such a long list of possible means of accessing the treatment (only one of which will work) that the child can't decide which way to go. All the while the parent insists that she loves the child. It will do the child little good to report that while he has a lot of worries about his choice of access, he nevertheless is committed to there being a right way to access his medical salvation. This is an odd situation existentially (even if it logically holds) and we might then ask what kind of parent would set things up that way.

To illustrate, let's grant that two thoughtful Christians, Mary and Joseph, have deeply conflicting views about how to get into the salvific relationship with Jesus. Suppose, further, that both Mary and Joseph hold to CSE as well as to salvific skepticism. Let's also assume that the two salvific views are explicitly contradictory; call them A and -A. For example, let's say Mary holds A, which is a "works" orientation and Joseph holds -A, which is a "faith alone" orientation. I'll assume that these two views are actually contradictory, as they seem on the surface to be, since one claims that at least some work must be done for one's salvation and the other that no work at all must (or can) be done. I assume here that faith is not a sort of "work." Starting with Joseph, let's suppose he reports that he (rationally) believes or knows -A. We already know that Joseph holds both CSE and salvific skepticism. However, his admission of all three positions creates an existential dilemma. CSE says that there is one true access to the salvific ontological order, but in order to protect that claim, salvific skepticism has been introduced. The salvific skepticism has created the epistemic safe haven Joseph seeks, but it does so by noting that it is irrelevant whether anyone really knows which access is right but that this doesn't remove the truth of the claim that there is a right access. Given the importance of the situation (one's salvation), won't one be motivated to check one's belief that one rationally believes or knows the right path? But so far forth, that only deals with the epistemology of the situation and while the epistemology is itself interesting, I want to concentrate on the existential results.

Let's grant the possibility that Joseph knows that -A (in other words, -A is true and he is in the right kind of situation such that believing -A is warranted for him). But Mary will potentially be in exactly the same situation. We could just as well grant that it is possible that she knows that A (A is true and she is in the right kind of situation so that her belief that A is warranted for her). But being salvific skeptics, it appears that the level of commitment to their respective knowledge claims (that they have the right salvific path) should be weaker and weaker. This, I propose, has the existential effect that any psychological certitude or sense of surety they feel about their salvation will be grossly undermined existentially. So while either one might actually know, they will (and arguably should) feel that something is deeply amiss. Mary and Joseph are at loggerheads about which is the right path and, from the salvific skepticism point of view, the retreat to salvific skepticism has protected CSE at the expense of what is existentially and religiously very important—feeling sure of one's own salvation.

I am not saying that the positions of other Christians serve as epistemic defeaters for one's own position on the salvific path. Plantinga and Alston both seem right when they argue, in their various ways, that the mere presence of other apparently warranted competitors to one's own beliefs does not entail that one doesn't know one's beliefs or rationally believe them.[5] Instead I'm suggesting that the issues discussed here raise the specter of a deep *existential crisis of faith* for some Christians. The location of that existential crisis falls, it seems, outside the "straight" epistemology of the situation into the realm of the extra-epistemological—the existential. Since we are emotional, psychological, and intuitive people, we should not overlook the role those aspects of our humanity have on our knowledge (or rational belief) and our claims to knowledge (or rational belief). But more importantly, for this discussion, we should not ignore the spiritual importance of the emotional, psychological, and intuitive. So while perhaps it is true that Joseph knows he is saved, he may very much begin to feel as if he doesn't know. Knowledge, one might say, is not all it's cracked up to be, at least in terms of living an existentially fulfilling religious life.

So, while there is a right way to achieve the appropriate relationship with Jesus, according to CSE as defended by salvific skepticism, one who holds to these views may not be in a position to have existential confidence about her knowledge concerning or belief in the right path. CSE defended by salvific skepticism seems to involve the existential result that one's *surety* of salvation can never be well-grounded. Insofar, finally, as this situation is rooted ultimately in God's salvific economy of love, it leaves one wondering about the wisdom of holding CSE.

Perhaps the salvific skeptic is willing to live with those results. Yet it seems she would pay a heavy price because the situation undermines the notion that God's grace is sufficient, not just for the afterlife, but for the very

---

5. Alston, *Perceiving God*, chapter 7 and Plantinga, "A Defense," 530.

important present. God's kingdom is the already/not-yet and not just the not-yet. Jesus was existentially concerned and involved with every person he met. He wasn't simply laying down a salvific guessing game. Thus, I believe that CSE, at least as defended by salvific skepticism, is best rejected. Yet insofar as a more or less radical separation between epistemology and metaphysics is rooted in descriptive realism, it seems that salvific skepticism is always lurking behind CSE's narrow gate. Thus, CSE is a view, although popularly and widely held (both directly and functionally), that should be discouraged in the actual lives of Christian believers. Taking a more open-access approach to how one should get onto the path with Jesus will be, I think, more consistent with Scripture and more helpful on an existential level. At the very least, if we teach our children that there is more than one way to access Jesus, perhaps we will see fewer crises of faith as they grow to adulthood. My personal experience engaging with many Christian college students is to find that they are often not able to embrace a wider sense of access to God's salvific call than the one with which they were raised. When they find the one with which they were raised problematic, they often take the closest door out of the church. Perhaps that existential result alone is enough to help us think about how we present the uniqueness of Jesus' work. Unique ontologically? Yes. Narrowly accessed? No.

The problem is similar to what I call "the existential problem of religious diversity."[6] The problem is not that one is unjustified in believing in Christianity when one discovers the rational faith of diversely other religious folk. As noted above, the discovery of other religious paths may provide some sort of question about the truth of one's own Christian belief, but that is not enough to make it irrational to continue on in one's faith. The problem is instead that one simply finds one's faith waning in the face of the diversity of religious belief; one finds oneself just not so sure that one's own path is the right one. One difference between that problem and the one I've tried to describe above is that in the existential problem of religious diversity it is the apparent rationality of other religious traditions that undermines one's faith. In the challenge outlined above, it is a problem inside the faith itself: one's evidence for one's self-surety about one's access to God in Christ through the Holy Spirit is just as rational, it seems, as the next Christian who has quite a different take on the matter. The rather strong sort of knowledge one would need to hold to CSE for oneself appears to be on shaky ground.

6. See McLeod-Harrison, *Repairing Eden*.

Chapter 4

Why We Should Preach the Gospel

The present chapter concentrates once again on the issue of human access to the gospel. Its focus is one sort of inclusivism, but its backdrop is an access exclusivism of the sort noted in the previous chapter. Christians sometimes think that there is only one (human) access to God's salvation and when they do, they are (all other things being equal) salvific exclusivists. The sort of inclusivism I discuss in this chapter is a narrow access inclusivism that tracks closely with exclusivism. Narrow inclusivism holds something like 1, 2, and 3*, where 3* is narrowly construed.

1. There is only one true description of reality, including salvific reality. The Christian description of salvific reality is that one true description.

2. The one true description of the Christian faith tells us that entering into a proper relationship with God through Jesus Christ through the power of the Holy Spirit is necessary and sufficient to be saved. Christ's incarnate work on earth—birth, death, resurrection—provide the monistic ontological basis for salvation.

3* More than one means can grant access to the proper salvific relationship to God through Jesus Christ and those means are disjunctively necessary and sufficient.

There is access to Christian salvation beyond the single access often thought to be the case (typically tied to a response to special revelation), but that access is usually limited to some sort of (narrow) response to general revelation.

It is often thought that the gospel must be preached in order that people can be saved. In fact, sermons that call people into missionary work sometimes take as their text Romans 10:14–15,

> But how are they to call on one in whom they have not believed? And how are they to believe in one of whom they have never heard? And how are they to hear without someone to proclaim him? And how are they to proclaim him unless they are sent? As it is written, "How beautiful are the feet of those who bring good news!"

Although often taken out of context (I take it up more fully in the excursus at the end of this chapter), this appears to be a straightforward call to preaching the gospel to those who won't be saved without it. Jesus too indicates that we should go into all the world, making disciples and baptizing in the name of the Father, Son, and Holy Spirit (Matt 28:18–20). One supposes that involves preaching the gospel as well.

The early apostles did just that, taking the gospel (by tradition, at least) to the ends (from their perspective) of the known world. The good news of Jesus Christ needed to be heard by everyone, for Christ's life amongst us, his death, resurrection, and ascension, were the means by which God, in provision for us all, invited us into the inner circle of divine love. Many a missionary and evangelist has understood the burden and blessing of preaching the good news to be rooted in a sort of exclusivism of the gospel message. But what of those who don't hear the gospel? Can they not be saved? The narrow access exclusivism of the gospel upon which much missionary work and preaching rests is often supplemented by another sort of access for those the missionaries and preachers don't reach. This chapter explores the narrow inclusivism that grows from these observations. That narrow access inclusivism is found wanting. My means of showing this is to ask the question, why should we preach the gospel? I use an essay written by William Lane Craig both to illustrate the narrow inclusivism and to explore the question of why we should preach.

Section I explains the position William Lane Craig takes—a narrow salvific inclusivism. Section II explains why such a position is untenable

Image, Incarnation, and Expansivism

and explores briefly some other issues surrounding narrow inclusivism. The chapter concludes with a brief excursus on Romans 10:14–15.

I

In "No Other Name,"[1] Craig takes up the question, "is there a problem with God's condemning those who do not follow Christ?" Specifically, he takes on challenges to the claim that salvation is provided by Christ exclusively. Craig's main point is to explore certain counterfactuals of freedom,[2] and while interesting and important, that is not my main concern. Instead I want to reflect directly on Craig's apparently narrow account of salvific inclusivism. What does he say and what does it imply? If the following argument is right, people who hold the sort of narrow inclusivism to which Craig seems committed should stop preaching, at least for the reason that people need to hear the gospel in order to be saved.

Craig claims that God loves humans and provides salvation from our fallen state. Jesus and his work—life, death, resurrection—are the basis for, and means to, God and the salvation provided by divine grace, which we receive by the power of the Holy Spirit. In brief, there is no other name through which salvation can occur but the name of Jesus. Thus far, we have a description of the salvific economy from an ontological point of view, reporting the facts about God's provision of salvation. This exclusivism, so far forth, is what we might think of as an *ontological* exclusivism; that is, if true, the description is exclusively true. There is no other name but Jesus' name by which one can be saved. Thus we avoid any sort of religious pluralism in terms of what is true about salvation. Among all the religions, the Christian message, rooted in God's self-disclosure in Jesus Christ and the Scriptures more broadly, is the one true account of the salvific economy. This harks back to the ontologically monistic component of CSE presented in chapter 1.

While Craig claims that Jesus is the access to God and the divine provision of salvation, he also seems committed to the view that humans must do something to receive it. We must respond to the gracious offer of salvation. If we do not, says Craig, we are condemned (having been condemned already in sin). Thus, Craig would, it seems, distinguish between *the work*

1. Craig, "No Other Name," 38–53.
2. "Counterfactuals of freedom" is philosopher's talk for alternative ways things might go based on human free choice. "What if Sally chooses against Christ instead of for?"

of Christ as the basis for salvation (which includes the divine access to God) and *the human access* to the work of Christ in a manner similar to what I suggested in chapter 1. It is natural, then, to ask how we can access or appropriate the work of Christ. Jesus is the path, so to speak, but how do we get onto the path? This harks back to 3, the access component, of CSE presented in chapter 1 and 3* at the beginning of this chapter.

Craig, like the Southern Baptist document quoted in chapter 1, would suggest that humans receive the gift of salvation by faith. Just how broad this notion of faith is, again, an open question. But as I suggested earlier, presumably it's not too open. One who had never heard of Jesus and perhaps didn't believe in God at all but who lived an exemplary good life would *not* be described as having personal faith in Jesus in the relevant sense. To be exclusivist about human access to God's salvation, one must think there are some limits on what "personal faith" comes to. Not just anything will count. If there are *no or very few limits*, such a view is not exclusive about access and one is more or less a *broad inclusivist* about access.[3] Under a broad inclusivist account, God could save people even when no faith in Christ was present. Thus, perhaps, faithful Buddhists, Muslims, Hindus, and so on could be saved by being included in God's provision of salvation through the life and work of Christ (thus the view remains ontologically exclusive about the basis of salvation, but inclusivist about human access). One supposes at death that a Buddhist included into Christian salvation would come to realize that it wasn't enlightenment she sought but a relationship with Jesus. At that point perhaps faith in Jesus would begin, yet that faith wouldn't provide the access (that she had by seeking enlightenment) but the way in which she went toward the truth (even though mis-describing it

---

3. In addition, there are all kinds of questions about when one must declare (or perhaps realize) one's personal faith—must it be before one throws off this mortal coil or is a post-death declaration possible? There is also an inclusivist gambit, mentioned in chapter 1, that might allow one to "have faith" without knowing one does. Alston "Referring" suggests that a person might refer to Christ or Christ's work via direct reference even when one is quite mistaken about the description of Christ. A Buddhist may refer to Christ when, for example, talking about enlightenment, even though a description of enlightenment will not accurately describe Jesus. A Buddhist might, therefore, be saved by "faith" and simply not know it. Such an account is not, one presumes, included in either the Southern Baptist notion of "personal faith" or in Craig's work. If that *is* what is meant by "personal faith" then effectively Craig would be completely on the side of inclusivism on human access and he should either stop preaching or preach for a different reason. See below.

Image, Incarnation, and Expansivism

during her earthly life).[4] A few more details are found later in this chapter about this possibility, but only a few. It is difficult for us to say how God thinks of these matters in detail. God doesn't look on our stature, but on our hearts, and it is a dangerous game to try to look fully into someone else's heart in terms of their salvific status before God. Nevertheless, the sort of position just described can be called "access-broadness" because there are few or no limits on what counts, in the end, as having personal faith. One can even have faith when one doesn't know one has.

The broad-access inclusivist would end up, one supposes, being broad in another sense as well. Not only are there no or few limits on what counts as personal faith but, because of that, it also seems plausible that many, perhaps the majority of folk from world history, will have accessed God's provision of salvation. If one takes the broad-access approach, perhaps one needs to "positively" reject any sense of goodness as a valuable goal for one's life in order to remain condemned. In rejecting goodness, one thereby rejects God. Perhaps there are few people who view (or have viewed) their lives in this way and therefore most people will be received by God in the end. Call this second sort of broadness, "result-broadness" because the resulting number of people who access God's provision of salvation is a large percentage of people (perhaps even everyone).

Here I turn directly to Craig's position. As noted, in one sense Craig seems to agree with the Southern Baptist statement on faith. Craig quotes a substantial number of biblical references that includes a mix of claims about the exclusivity of salvation on the basis of Christ alone, along with claims about believing in Jesus (or the work thereof) as the human access to salvation. Craig seems to think that a reflective decision for or against Jesus (presumably leading to faith in Christ or away from faith in Christ) is the access point to salvation.

Craig, however, is somewhat more inclusivist in his approach than the Southern Baptist document allows. It does not explicitly allow for any other access than that available through overt faith in Jesus as Lord. Craig does. He suggests that some people (Old Testament saints, for example) can access salvation *even when they don't know they are doing it*.[5] The Old

---

4. It is probably a bit of a mis-description to call post-mortem faith "faith." In the kingdom, faith and hope will pass away, but not charity. One supposes that those who would be included in the kingdom via the inclusivist account given would have the same status in God's presence as the hardiest Christian follower.

5. Craig is a little cautious when he writes about this, saying "one could maintain." If he doesn't actually maintain the view in question, or something like it, my argument

Testament saints cannot be said to have had faith in Jesus as Lord when, indeed, they had never even heard of Jesus and most likely would not have recognized him as Lord (any more than many faithful Jews at Jesus' time did). I'm assuming, here, that to have faith in Jesus as Lord one must be *aware* that one has faith in Jesus as Lord. But not everyone is aware that they are accessing the work of Christ as they are saved. So Craig is an inclusivist about human access to God's provision of salvation.

But he is, in one sense at least, *narrowly* inclusivist. Craig lists a variety of biblical verses in support of the claim that the vast majority of humanity will be condemned to hell on the basis of their sin. These folk either reject belief in Christ or fail to respond appropriately to general revelation. So even though open to the possibility that some will access the work of Christ without even knowing they are doing so, Craig thinks this happens relatively infrequently. Even when someone is fully aware of the gospel message, the percentage of people who respond in faith to Jesus as Lord is small. The gate truly is narrow, in Craig's understanding. Craig clearly takes the Christian Scriptures to teach not only that the work of Jesus Christ is the only basis in virtue of which salvation occurs (when it does), but that most humans—including those who adhere to non-Christian religions—do not avail themselves of that salvation by an appropriate belief or action (faith) and therefore remain condemned to hell. So Craig's access inclusivism is narrow in result. He clearly rejects result-broadness.

Is his view also narrow in the access sense? That is much more difficult to say and Craig would need to be more forthcoming for us to tell. But we might surmise that it is narrow in the access sense of inclusivism as well because of the fact that Craig believes so few enter the kingdom at all. If he took a broad-access view of inclusivism one would suppose he would end up with a broad-result inclusivism as well.

The burden of Craig's paper is to respond to those who find the Christian exclusivity of salvation problematic. In trying to locate the problem, Craig writes:

> But what exactly is the problem with God's condemning persons who adhere to non-Christian religions? I do not see that the very notion of hell is incompatible with a just and loving God. According to the New Testament, God does not want anyone to perish, but desires that all persons repent and be saved and come to know

doesn't go through. But then, Craig does seem to need an explanation, then, for those Old Testament saints and for those who have never heard the gospel.

> the truth.... He therefore seeks to draw all men [sic] to Himself. Those who make a well-informed and free decision to reject Christ are self-condemned, since they repudiate God's unique sacrifice for sin. By spurning God's prevenient grace and the solicitations of His Spirit, they shut out God's mercy and seal their own destiny. They, therefore, and not God, are responsible for their condemnation, and God deeply mourns their loss. Nor does it seem to me that the problem can be simply reduced to the inconsistency of a loving and just God's condemning persons who are either un-, ill-, or misinformed concerning Christ and who therefore lack the opportunity to receive Him. For one could maintain that God graciously applies to such persons the benefits of Christ's atoning death without their conscious knowledge thereof on the basis of their response to the light of general revelation and the truth that they do have, even as He did in the case of Old Testament figures like Job who were outside the covenant of Israel. The testimony of Scripture is that the mass of humanity do not even respond to the light that they do have, and God's condemnation of them is neither unloving nor unjust, since He judges them according to standards of general revelation vastly lower than those which are applied to persons who have been recipients of His special revelation.[6]

As I noted above, Craig goes on to state that the real problem with Christian exclusivism, as he sees it, is with certain counterfactuals of freedom. He provides a detailed response to that problem. My interest lies, for the most part, elsewhere, viz., on what Craig thinks about human access to the divine salvific economy.

He says the following: "Those who make a well-informed and free decision to reject Christ are self-condemned, since they repudiate God's unique sacrifice for sin." One presumes that if a well-informed and free decision to reject Christ is enough to self-condemn (given sin), then a well-informed and free choice to accept Christ supplies access to God's provision of salvation. Let's call this "special revelation access" or SRA. As to the second means of access—what we can call "general revelation access" or GRA—we might also surmise that a free choice is involved either toward one's salvation or toward one's condemnation. It is a choice to respond positively (or negatively) to the light one has. Here one is uninformed about Christ and yet well-informed enough about God (or more ambiguously, the "salvific other") from general revelation that one could freely and thoughtfully respond to the light one has. Of course, the GRA sort of choice may

6 Ibid., 42.

not be as immediate or dramatic as responding to an altar call, but it nevertheless involves a choice. So with both SRA and GRA, free choice and thought is involved.

In GRA, however, Craig says that the standards are vastly lower than in SRA. Now which standards he has in mind are left open. At least two sorts of possibility suggest themselves. First, the decision to follow Christ may require more of a person than the decision to follow the light. Perhaps once one hears and understands the gospel message, one's choice toward Christ will set one on a more demanding moral and spiritual path than if one merely responds to the light of general revelation. One's following the light one has may entail that God's moral and spiritual expectations are, simply, lower than for the one who hears the (whole) gospel message. On SRA, one simply has more clear information on which to act. On this reading she who responds to the light (not having heard the gospel) makes a decision to follow the light, but presumably what is important is not only the decision to follow but the *successful* following (where by "successful" I mean that God has certain rules or morals she must obey). The Christian, too, on this take, has certain things she must do (beyond the decision to have faith in Christ) in order to succeed in a faithful manner leading to salvific access.

I reject this interpretation, and I suspect Craig would too, for it seems to make something beyond personal faith necessary for accessing salvation. Not only must one believe on the Lord Jesus Christ (or, on GRA, believe in God, go toward the light in trust, etc.), but one must do some good works, develop spiritually, and so forth. The water in this pool gets a little murky, however. One has to ask about the relationship of justification and sanctification, for example. If one accepts Jesus as Lord on one's deathbed, and has little time to develop one's moral and spiritual muscles, does that keep one from accessing salvation? I think Craig would say "no." Our access to salvation should not be turned into a works-righteousness. While faith without works is dead, one still accesses salvation by faith and not by works. If one has a deathbed faith, and little works to show, one still has faith, even if, should one survive one's deathbed experience, one should grow in one's faith by works. Sanctification is not justification.[7]

---

7. This is a particularly Protestant account of the relationship of justification and sanctification, perhaps. My own view is more complicated. James's emphasis on faith without works being dead points us toward thinking holistically about our lives as humans. Faith and faithfulness are two sides of the same coin. One can't really have one without the other. So it's not "faith plus works" so much as faith manifest in works and

Image, Incarnation, and Expansivism

The second interpretation is more likely. It suggests that the information on which one is making a GRA choice pro or con is less clear than the information given in SRA. One supposes that God makes it easier to go through the GRA gate because more guesswork is needed on the part of the humans involved. The bar is lower, hence, not because less is expected of one's moral or spiritual life (whether on SRA and GRA, one is expected to actually follow through, given one's information, with becoming a better person, for example) but because the epistemic situation is vaguer on GRA than on SRA. One can be excused more easily for passing through a stop light when one is driving in an Ontario white-out than if you have a clear view of the traffic light. There are degrees, here, too. The more blinding the storm, the more likely one will be let off. A few snowflakes won't let you off. Still, decisions are made on the basis of the light given.[8]

But even here things are not entirely clear. One might be expected to believe and trust in God for salvation whereas on SRA one is expected to believe more specifically in Jesus, perhaps. It is a little hard to say exactly what the difference will be in belief content. Perhaps an animist who truly follows the animist belief system will meet God's minimalist standards whereas an unfaithful animist will not. Or perhaps there might be an animist who is mistaken about her animist beliefs (that is, she is mistaken about what animism teaches) and thinks the spiritual reality is not in the animal spirits but a singular spirit behind the animals. Or perhaps it isn't belief *per se* that is important but a general sort of trust that ultimate reality (which admittedly is pretty mysterious) will save one from the vagaries of the situation in which one finds oneself. But let's say God does have specific criteria in mind for GRA and God knows how to apply them. In the end (post-mortem) such people will presumably know that the salvific basis is, in fact, Jesus. The saved animist will simply come to know the truth more accurately and fully.

---

work manifest in faith. While I believe human access is through faith, faith itself is a sort of work one does. So I suggest that there is a continuum of faith/works that does not have a purely "faith alone" component nor, perhaps, a purely "work alone" component. Suggesting such a position does not undermine that it is one's faith that grants access (on the human side) to the gift of salvation. The faith I have in mind, however, is not a works-righteousness sort of faith, for Jesus has done all the work needed on the divine side to provide salvation for us.

8. And a host of other factors as well. Perhaps such things as intelligence play a role, or emotional stability or, more likely according to the Gospels, the more childlike one is in responding. The same is true, presumably, of SRA and GRA in this regard.

II

Here we finally reach a point where we can say why people who hold the narrow inclusivism that Craig suggests should stop preaching. Presumably Craig has in mind (something close to) the second interpretation, since the difference between special and general revelation seems to be substantially about the information provided. Since it is easier in GRA to obtain access than in SRA, it seems to follow that more people will gain access by GRA than SRA. Consider an analogy. Suppose there are one hundred people. Suppose further that it is easier to obtain a winning lottery ticket at a store than by standing outside the lottery headquarters. Finally, suppose either everyone goes to a store or everyone goes the headquarters, but not both. If everyone goes to the store, more people are going to get a winning lottery ticket than if everyone goes to the headquarters. Think of accessing salvation through GRA as akin to getting hold of the winning lottery ticket at the store and accessing salvation through SRA as akin to obtaining it at the headquarters. On this analysis, holders of narrow inclusivism should stop preaching as it seems that a greater number of people will find salvation (the winning lottery ticket) if they don't have SRA.

Now the case is, in fact, more complicated than that. For the choice isn't between everyone going to a store vs. everyone going to headquarters. Rather, it is that everyone goes to the store first and some people also go headquarters. The set of people who see the light and could respond includes everyone. They have a (relatively) easy way to access salvation. Is the preaching of the gospel helping anyone under this scenario? If a person hasn't already responded to the light of nature in the (relatively) easy way to access salvation, what help is there for those who hear Craig's sermons? For them, the bar is just made higher and there is no going back. They cannot "unhear" the SRA. Once one goes to the lottery headquarters one cannot go back to the easier access of the store. This, in some way, seems worse than where everyone either has GRA or everyone has SRA. At least in those conditions, everyone has the same chance of accessing salvation. They either get it from the light or they get it from the preaching, but not both. On the scenario where only some hear the preaching, they are in worse shape—are less likely to gain access to salvation—than those who never hear. Again, the preaching should stop.

But it seems that there are further problems lurking in the narrow inclusivism neighborhood. Here I want to quote something from near the end of Craig's essay. At this point in the paper, Craig has developed a

Molinist account of counterfactuals of freedom and applied it to the choices humans make in response to SRA and GRA.[9] He attempts on that basis to show that God's love for us and his provision of salvation is consistent with the fact that the vast majority of people die in their sin. He lists three possibilities intended to show the consistency. The third of these answers this question: "Why did God not supply special revelation to persons who, while rejecting the general revelation they do have, would have responded to the gospel of Christ if they had been sufficiently well-informed concerning it?"[10] His answer?

> There are no such persons. In each world in which they exist God loves and wills the salvation of persons who in the actual world have only general revelation, and He graciously and preveniently solicits their response by His Holy Spirit, but in every world feasible for God they freely reject His grace and are lost. If there were anyone who would have responded to the gospel if he had heard it, then God in His love would have brought the gospel to such a person. Apart from miraculous intervention, "a single revelation to the whole earth has never in the past been possible, given the facts of geography and technology"; but God in His providence has so arranged the world that as the gospel spread outward from its historical roots in first-century Palestine, all who would respond to this gospel, were they to hear it, did and do hear it. Those who have only general revelation and do not respond to it would also not have responded to the gospel had they heard it. Hence, no one is lost because of lack of information due to historical or geographical accident. All who want or would want to be saved will be saved.[11]

In the second sentence, Craig says "If there were anyone who would have responded to the gospel if he had heard it, then God in His love would have brought the gospel to such a person." I wonder what this claim comes to. Would there ever be a need for God to bring the gospel to such a person? Apparently not, for such a person would already have responded to GRA.

---

9. Molinism is a view developed to explain how God can be omniscient and hence know all truths about the future while not interfering with human freedom. On Molinism, God knows all the future possible acts of every human (the counterfactuals of freedom, as philosophers call them) and knows which of those acts any given person will do under each and every set of circumstances in which she may find herself. Thus, God knows right now all future contingents and yet doesn't interfere with human choice.

10. Ibid., 51.

11. Ibid.

In the second to the last sentence Craig says that if one doesn't respond to GRA then one also will not respond to SRA. His point is that in all the worlds God could feasibly make, the humans who would reject salvific access freely do reject salvific access. God can't change that. So, the fact that some people only receive GRA does not suggest that God is unfair for, given certain counterfactuals of freedom, those who don't respond positively to GRA would not, in fact, respond positively to SRA. That is part of the burden of Craig's paper, viz., to show that Christianity's claim to be the exclusive means of salvation is not, in fact, unfair. It's not unfair, basically, because everyone has access to salvation via GRA. The fact that so many are condemned to hell is not ever the result of not having heard the gospel. Those who never hear the gospel would not have responded positively to it had they heard it. Craig's explanation falls out of his analysis of the counterfactual situations.

What I'm interested in is not so much the counterfactual argument but one result of it. If my reading of Craig's position is right, the counterfactual in the quoted passage can serve as a premise in the following argument: If one has only GRA and does not respond to it, then one would not respond to SRA had it been offered. But suppose one is offered SRA and responds to it. It follows that one would also respond to unadorned GRA. On this argument, one responds to GRA *in any case* and would have whether or not one has SRA. Thus, no one would ever need to hear the gospel, as a matter of fact. Craig's inclusivism is much wider than he seems to think because, in fact, it doesn't matter whether the gospel is preached. Those who would be saved via preaching would have also been saved via GRA. People holding a Craig-like position should quit preaching, this time not because it makes things more difficult, but because one could do more useful things, like writing philosophy, perhaps, or spending more time with one's family or working in a soup kitchen.

This, in turn, makes perfectly good sense, given Craig's view that GRA has a lower bar than SRA. Of course, with counterfactuals of freedom, one need not think of causal relationships between the antecedent and consequent. There is nothing in Craig's essay that would lead one to think that Craig makes a causal link between the two. Nevertheless, one might wonder whether, in the actual world, his claim that the bar is lower on GRA shows that one's failing to respond to the light provides at least certain causal aspects for failing also to respond to preaching. Any reason one would have that leads to one positively responding to the preaching, one also would

Image, Incarnation, and Expansivism

have for responding to the light. Surely no one who wouldn't pass the lower would pass the higher. Since everyone has the lower bar in front of her, no one need preach the higher bar.

There is another interesting point about this last quotation, viz., Craig's calling attention to the possibility of a miraculous revelation where everyone hears about SRA. What if, by some miraculous intervention on God's part, everyone could hear the world's finest evangelistic sermon? Under such conditions, no one would be left only to the light. Then everyone would have exactly the same opportunity to respond and in the same conditions. But again, more people are likely to access salvation through GRA than SRA and people holding narrow inclusivism should not preach, even if they could reach everyone all at once with the gospel message. Looked at from another vantage point, however, preaching to everyone would make no difference. The set of folk who are saved remains exactly the same whether one preaches or not. Preaching does not increase the number who would be saved. So there appears to be a sort of dilemma for preaching. It either makes it more difficult for people to access salvation, in which case one should (morally) stop preaching, or exactly the same people will be saved whether anyone preaches or not, in which case we should spend our time more productively.

Another odd result is indicated by Craig's analysis. The very people who would be saved are saved. That is the logic of the counterfactuals of freedom to which Craig appeals. So far so good. Yet it strikes me as strange that for the most part, people in the far reaches of the East, southern Africa, and North and South America all fall into the camp of not needing the gospel preached to them, given the historical pattern of evangelism. God in his providence, Craig says, so arranged the world that as the gospel spread out from Palestine all who would respond to the gospel, were they to hear it, did and do hear it. It seems to follow that the counterfactuals of freedom fall along geographical lines. Those in Europe, at least up until the missionary movements of the sixteenth and nineteenth centuries, fall into the camp of those who would respond in faith, if they heard the gospel. Those outside Europe did not fall into that group, given the historic pattern of evangelism. Of course, some from non-European civilizations would still be saved, according the Craig's logic, for they could respond to GRA and its lower bar. But surely, given that human nature is the same everywhere, roughly similar numbers of people from non-European settings would have responded to the gospel had they heard it. It seems odd that all of sudden (in the sixteenth or nineteenth centuries) people from non-European societies would become more likely to respond the gospel were it preached to them than they were up until that point in history. While one supposes it is *possible* that Craig's account is true, it seems sociologically odd. Does reading the history as providential here smack of racial or cultural bias? To avoid such bias, which I'm sure Craig would want to do, doesn't he need to admit that just as many folk who never heard the gospel for the first sixteen hundred years came to salvation via GRA as did in Europe under SRA? But then, once again, what's the point of preaching the gospel? What is the advantage from the point of view of salvific access?

There are two potential sources of the problem facing the narrow inclusivist position. One is the ranking of the means of access. So long as even one more person can access salvation on GRA rather than SRA (because it is easier to do so), then the preaching should stop. If we were to reverse the difficulty of access—*per impossible* have a lower bar for SRA than GRA—would that let the narrow inclusivist preach? Perhaps. The preaching would set a lower bar, but then everyone would eventually get the higher bar as a backup. That's ok. But then the problem is that the narrow inclusivist is obligated to preach to everyone. The SRA bar is lower and therefore creates an obligation for the easier path to be accessible to all. In effect, that is the role of GRA—to give everyone a chance to respond positively to God. Perhaps, indeed, many evangelists and missionaries think that they should preach to everyone because the bar is set lower, given their preaching. That is why they are motivated to do what they do. But it seems impossible to reverse the difficulty of access. The reason access is easier on GRA is that GRA leaves people with more vague (or perhaps less) information and presumably God lets more through the gate because of that. What is expected of such folk is to respond as well as they can but enough to indicate that they have decided to go toward the light rather than away from it. With SRA, the decision is based on much more clear grounds and therefore the person with SRA has a more difficult time. To whom much is given, much is expected. One has to respond with faith in Jesus and no groping to find one's way is allowed any "extra" grace. So long as the gate provided by SRA is harder to get through than the gate provided by GRA, the narrow inclusivist shouldn't preach.

Another source of the problem, however, may just be the introduction of the inclusiveness in the first place. Without it, the narrow inclusivist could preach and we would have a quite complete salvific exclusivism. Not only would the nature of Christ's work be exclusive, but there would only be one means of accessing it on the human side, viz., SRA. Once the salvific exclusivist preaches, the person hearing can decide. Without the preaching, God's hands, it seems, would be tied and no one would have SRA and hence no one could come to salvation. Of course, one might appeal to the counterfactuals of freedom in such a way that the very people who would respond to the gospel are given the opportunity to respond. God in his love for people would arrange for the gospel to be preached to those who would respond if they heard it. But to keep things fair, it seems that everyone would need to hear the gospel, there being no GRA. Everyone would need a chance to turn God's offer down or accept it. Here, of course, we are back to the apparent necessity of preaching to everyone. Again, this has perhaps been the motivation for many a missionary and evangelist. But of course, no one can reach everyone and, thus far, probably not even the whole force of the church has reached everyone.

If Craig did hold such a view (which he does not), then it would be natural to ask him why he does. Such a view seems terribly harsh. There are all those Old Testament saints to deal with, and millions of untold folk who never heard because they were born before Christ or are raised in another religion or no religion at all. Craig's answer, in the essay in question, is that only those who would respond will respond. Thus, on the narrow inclusivist's account, the gospel only needs to be preached to those who will respond in order for some to be saved. But given the requirements of fairness—that in the end everyone is responsible for the *actual* decisions she makes—everyone needs an opportunity to turn Jesus down. One cannot do that without preaching to all or by having GRA. Without GRA, the narrow inclusivist's account collapses. But if that is true, and there is a lower standard God can and does use, then the preaching should end. Once the door is open to include everyone in the world via GRA, the narrow inclusivist shouldn't preach at all.

Would it help if the bar is not set lower for GRA but set at the same level as SRA? Should the preaching go on then? If the narrow inclusivist is not making the bar higher, then, while she or he would (finally) be permitted to preach, it's not clear *why* she or he should. The time should be spent, perhaps, more wisely.

It seems that there are two ways the narrow inclusivist might respond to the argument. The first is to simply remove the suggestion that GRA has a much lower bar than SRA. The suggested response says that the narrow

Why We Should Preach the Gospel

inclusivist should argue that, in fact, SRA makes it easier to respond to the gospel. Human beings are (in part) rational beings. We want to understand the things to which we commit ourselves. When we don't understand them, we at least reassure ourselves that other people do understand them and that we can trust those people. Now it seems far easier—because far more intellectually satisfying—to have trusting faith in God when one has some knowledge of the content of the Christian faith. If this is right, then having faith in God is easier for those under SRA than those under GRA.[12] Call this the "easy-SRA response."

Should the narrow inclusivist keep preaching the gospel because such preaching makes it easier for people to believe in God? Perhaps, if that is all there is to the relative difficulty of coming into a saving relationship with Christ. But there is a lot more to the situation. The easy-SRA response, first of all, confuses ease of getting over the bar with intellectual satisfaction. Indeed, intellectual satisfaction might come at great expense in terms of the difficulty of understanding something. Sometimes it is easier to get over a bar simply by trusting that someone else knows what's going on. Little children do this all the time. Their parents tell them the doctor can be trusted, the child goes along. Meanwhile, the parents are struggling to figure out if, indeed, the doctor is seeing the whole picture. But maybe that response works because it is children we are talking about and not adults. Adults might find it easier to believe or trust when they understand. I think that generally true. But it misses the mark in another way. The bar of salvation is easier to get over because the intellectual situation is vaguer. It may very well be that the strength of one's faith (in the light, God, etc.) needed by someone with only GRA is quite small because of intellectual vagaries, whereas with the full Jesus story the strength of faith is much stronger or more difficult to maintain, etc. The point is, however, that it is not, in the end, all that clear that Craig, or anyone else, knows what it means to say that the bar is lower with GRA than with SRA. The actual criteria for accessing salvation is not all that clear in Scripture, with a variety of descriptions in various contexts. Jesus says a number of different things: come, follow me, unless you are born again, I am the Messiah, go sell everything you have and give it to the poor, etc. And these are all spoken to people *prior to* his work on the cross and in the resurrection. Exactly which, if any, of these

---

12. This approach to why it may be easier for SRA than GRA was suggested to me by Phil Smith. I thank him for some helpful comments on this chapter overall.

should we take as a model for what constitutes good access to the saving work of Jesus?

At this point, one might say that the narrow inclusivist should keep preaching because the Bible tells him to preach. One sometimes hears this sort of position taken on motivating missionary endeavors. Perhaps it is the right one. Yet shouldn't we want more than just a sort of raw command? Wouldn't it be good to preach when one has a reason to preach other than being told to do it? In response, one might say, "well, it is God who is telling us to preach; our call as Christians is to be faithful, not necessarily to understand why, in every instance." Such a fideistic response, however, seems inappropriate or at least intellectually unmotivated. There is another sort of reason to preach, and that brings me to the second response the narrow inclusivist might take.

The narrow inclusivist should preach *for a different reason*. Instead of needing to preach to bring people to Christ for salvation, maybe she just needs to preach to help people know more—in short, to know whereof their salvation arises. Since I am not against preaching the gospel, and since I've done it myself, it would be odd for me to suggest that we not preach at all. In fact, there are aspects of narrow inclusivist's evangelistic efforts I admire. Those aspects do not include, however, the underpinnings of the evangelism as I think it is often understood. I believe people do need to know about Jesus and the work he has done, work that provides us access to God's salvation. But that is not because I think they will go to hell if they don't respond to the preached gospel. Perhaps they will, but that, it seems to me, is another matter best left entirely up to God. I believe, however, that everyone is covered by God's inclusive love and provision of salvation. I'm just not sure who or under what conditions a given person can access it. Rather, I think we should preach because a fuller account of the truth will enable people to engage more easily with the God who loves them, at least in most cases.[13] And I believe the truth will set them free—free to worship more thoughtfully, more gratefully, and more knowledgeably.

There is an additional reason why I think we should preach the gospel for knowledge's sake rather than to provide people access to salvation. It seems that Craig's particular position is made worse by his commitment to the idea that the vast majority of people will spend eternity in hell.

---

13. It seems to me that sometimes preaching the gospel is best left to our actions rather than our words. Sometimes people have been wounded by the church and the best way to encourage them into a better relationship with God through Jesus is by loving them. Words don't always love, even when they are true.

While understanding that Craig is committed to this view as the biblical account, I think the view is too harsh and, in fact, not as clearly biblical as Craig believes. When Jesus speaks of hell, he virtually always is talking to the religious leadership and not the vast masses of people to whom he preached.[14] One might surmise that in Jesus' mind, hell was largely reserved for religious hypocrites who required more of the average person than the Scripture itself seemed to teach. And while Paul and John talk a lot about salvation, there isn't so much talk about hell, except in the revelation of John. But in that rather mysterious book, hell is cast into the lake of fire, an indication, perhaps, that hell is not going to last forever. So while it is possible, certainly, that some people will continue on in hell, it is not clear that this should be our focus in evangelism nor that Scripture promotes the idea as clearly as the tradition has it. I suggest that Dante's Inferno does more to promote the idea than does Scripture. While I certainly think people can, in the end, rebel against God and remove themselves from God's loving presence, I don't view hell as a place of punishment and wrath. Rather, it is a mournful place where, as Dostoevsky's Father Zosima says, people have become incapable of love.[15]

I think that a good case can be made for a much broader view of the number of people who will obtain salvation—a broad-result inclusivism. I would add, however, that perhaps we Christian philosophers and theologians need to consider not only the text of the Bible but the actual concrete situations of people and how they live their lives. Faithfulness to the light that people have been given may make for *both* easier access (broad-access inclusivism) and *also* for a much larger percentage of people entering the kingdom than Craig seems to allow (broad-result inclusivism). This goes to the point I made earlier about the so-called "providential" distribution of people who would believe if only they heard. Perhaps GRA is enough for salvation to be accessed across the board and SRA merely explains to people what the truth of the matter actually is.

But there is also a moral point with an underlying logical feature that connects Craig's few-people-get-to-heaven viewpoint with why he should stop preaching for the reasons he does. Perhaps, indeed, there are so few people who are going to arrive in heaven precisely because of preaching

---

14. This was pointed out to me by Susan McLeod-Harrison.

15. The topic of hell and the Christian eschaton is far more complicated than I can enter into in any detail here. To whet one's theological appetite, however, one might consider the following: Date, Stump, and Anderson, eds, *Rethinking Hell*; Date and Highfield, eds., *A Consuming Passion*; Walls, *Hell: The Logic of Damnation*.

efforts. If, in fact, preaching actually makes it harder for people to get to heaven then preaching actually reduces the number of people who will make it heaven. The more preaching that occurs, the fewer the people who will find salvation. This is precisely, one supposes, contrary to the way many people think of evangelistic and missionary efforts. While believing that preachers and missionaries act out of love (preaching brings people into the kingdom), preaching actually *reduces* the number, thus showing that the love that motivates it is ill-approached. True love would lead evangelists and missionaries *not* to preach or engage in evangelistic missionary work for the "saving of souls." Of course, if Craig's analysis of transworld damnation is correct, perhaps no fewer or no more people will get into heaven anyway.[16] Only those who would, will. But that too, seems to undermine preaching. If only those who would not, will not, then one wonders why one should preach anyway. Those who would, presumably, also will. Just as there are those who are transworld damned, there are also those who are transworld saved. Won't they be saved whether the gospel is preached to them or not? Won't they be inclined to say yes to God even without hearing the gospel?

Craig, in opening up the notion of an inclusive access to God's gracious provision of salvation, already indicates a certain sort of openness to a less harsh view. I find it interesting that Craig ends his essay with this:

> I hope that no reader has been offended by what might appear to be a rather dry and dispassionate discussion of the salvation and damnation of people apart from Christ. But with such an emotionally explosive issue on the table, it seems to me that it is prudent to treat it with reserve. No orthodox Christian *likes* the doctrine of hell or delights in anyone's condemnation. I truly wish that universalism were true, but it is not. My compassion toward those in other world religions is therefore expressed, not in pretending that

---

16. Craig's notion of transworld damnation is a result of his analysis of counterfactuals of freedom and God's knowledge of them. In short, the idea is that God knows all the possible ways any given person could possibly choose to act under any given set of conditions. So, God knows that any given person P will choose to reject God's salvation no matter what the circumstances. So humans are free and yet God knows who will be saved and who will not be saved. Some will choose against God no matter what circumstances (no matter what "possible world" hence the term "transworld") they find themselves in and hence will not be saved. These are the people with the property of "transworld damnation." The idea is that people are free to choose as they will, that some will freely choose against God no matter what, and those people will be damned. Yet God knows ahead of time which people will be saved and which will not, as a matter of fact, no matter what the possible circumstances, freely turn to God and reject damnation.

they are not lost and dying without Christ, but by my supporting and making every effort myself to communicate to them the life-giving message of salvation through Christ.[17]

A few last reflections on this quotation will make my point. First, it is not clear that orthodoxy requires belief in hell as a permanent resting place for humans who do not turn to Christ in this life. The historic creeds (Apostles' and Nicene) talk about salvation, but not hell. Craig speaks, in fact, of Vatican II having moved away from the exclusive message of Christ. It seems to me, however, that the position of the Roman Church is an inclusivist position about access, rather than inclusivist about the basis of salvation.

Second, while I honor Craig's commitment to the authority of Scripture, I wonder if perhaps he should pay a little closer attention to his own admitted propensities to wish the door to swing it a little wider ajar, even if not all the way to universalism. Orthodoxy need not require that the vast majority of people go to hell, even if the church has historically held that hell is the resting place for those who do not turn to Christ. But having said that, I also find it surprising that Craig brings up universalism in the context of his essay, for one can be an inclusivist about salvific access without being a universalist. But he did bring it up.

He says, in fact, no orthodox Christian likes the doctrine of hell. This, it seems, is an empirical claim that is false. Consider Jonathan Edwards's sometimes-extreme Calvinism whose logic includes the idea that the elect will, once in heaven, join God in his righteous condemnation of those in hell.[18] The elect will, in effect, celebrate that justice is done. While not exactly a statement that we should *like* the doctrine of hell, celebrating that "justice is done" is close to bordering on it, rather like being glad to see a person hung because justice is done.

Should we like the doctrine of hell? Probably not. Should God? That, of course, gets back at the heart of Craig's paper, the point of which is to show that, in the end, God can do nothing about the fact that humans have condemned themselves to hell and there, but for the grace of God, go I. The question remains, how wide is that grace? Craig says God mourns the loss of those in hell, but God's hands are effectively tied by the counterfactuals of human freedom. Perhaps they are, in the end. Humans can, of course, want to be separated from God and may, in the end, desire hell more than

17 Ibid., 53.
18 See Edwards, "The End of the Wicked."

they desire love. That is a choice we can make. But nothing in the logic of that choice shows that the vast majority of us end up in hell. The "plain teaching" of Scripture on the matter is not as plain as it has sometimes been thought. Grace freely offered is not, of course, grace freely received. Some may decide against it. How many? Of that I am quite unsure. That Craig himself wishes universalism were true indicates, perhaps, that he isn't so sure either. Craig's motivation for preaching, hence, may be better off in the realm of helping people see the fuller picture of God's grace than in connection to granting a different sort of access than GRA. In sum, given that the fact (if it is a fact) that those who would be saved will be saved and the fact that GRA gives an easier and therefore more productive approach to salvation, it seems that the narrow inclusivist should stop preaching unless the motivation for doing it changes.

EXCURSUS ON ROMANS 10:11–17

Romans 10:11–17 is sometimes used to defend, biblically, the preaching of the gospel as well as to suggest that without preaching many will miss the opportunity to be saved. It says:

> The Scripture says, "No one who believes in him will be put to shame." For there is no distinction between Jew and Greek; the same Lord is Lord of all and is generous to all who call on him. For, "Everyone who calls on the name of the Lord shall be saved." But how are they to call on one in whom they have not believed? And how are they to believe in one of whom they have never heard? And how are they to hear without someone to proclaim him? And how are they to proclaim him unless they are sent? As it is written, "How beautiful are the feet of those who bring good news!" But not all have obeyed the good news; for Isaiah says, "Lord, who has believed our message?" So faith comes from what is heard, and what is heard comes through the word of Christ.

Paul is teaching, among other things, that if you believe in Christ, you will not be ashamed; if you call on his name, you will be saved. It doesn't matter if you are Jew or Greek. The gospel is open to all. He further says that one can't call on Christ for salvation if one hasn't heard of Christ and one can't hear of Christ unless one receives the word through preaching. Faith comes from what is heard (at least potentially, for not all believe) and what is heard comes from preaching Christ. This passage, in short, sounds fairly exclusivistic, not only in terms of Christ and his work, but also in terms of human access to that work. However, it is interesting that the two statements dealing with human access (one about belief, another about calling) appear to be statements of *sufficiency rather than necessity*. If one believes, one will not be put to shame; if one calls on Jesus name, then one will be saved. Getting an exclusivistic access out of this passage seems difficult, given that observation.

It would be too quick to read the passage as exclusivistic in access for two other reasons as well. First, Paul is struggling with the relationship of the gospel given to the Gentiles and the law as given to the Jews. He later says that all of Israel will be saved (Rom 11:25–31) and he does so in the context of the difficult doctrine of election. The Jews will be saved, it appears, even if they do not believe in this life. That is consonant with the fact that believing in this life is sufficient for salvation and with Paul's lack of mention of the necessity of belief for salvation in this life. Second, Paul indicates that some are saved even if they do not hear or seek salvation. Romans 10:18–21 says:

> But I ask, have they not heard? Indeed they have; for "Their voice has gone out to all the earth, and their words to the ends of the world." Again I ask, did Israel not understand? First Moses says, "I will make you jealous of those who are not a nation; with a foolish nation I will make you angry." Then Isaiah is so bold as to say, "I have been found by those who did not seek me; I have shown myself to those who did not ask for me." But of Israel he says, "All day long I have held out my hands to a disobedient and contrary people."

This is a difficult passage and it seems to be best made sense of by Paul taking the quotations to be prophetic. That is, Moses and Isaiah were talking, when they wrote, about the future state of events that are happening at the time of Christ. Taken that way, the gist of it seems to be that the Gentiles do hear: "Their voice has gone out to all the earth, their words to the ends of the world." The larger context indicates that the gospel goes to the Gentiles in order to make the Jews jealous and hence turn to the gospel of Christ rather than the law as the source of salvation. The Gentiles, who did not seek God, find him; those who did not receive the law, receive salvation. Yet Israel, who have the law, are disobedient and reject Christ.

The burden of Paul's message in Romans 9, 10, and 11 is to explain, so far as he can, the mysteries of God's work of salvation among the Jews and

Image, Incarnation, and Expansivism

Gentiles. One group has the truth (special revelation) and another doesn't, but the group with the special revelation fails to live up to the law they are given. On the other side of the coin, however, the group without special revelation embraces what they do not even seek. Yet even more difficult, Israel is the elect of God and is saved in the end! God apparently hardens the hearts of Israel so the gospel will be preached to the Gentiles. Yet when the elect is full (among the Gentiles), all Israel will be saved.

In short, the ways by which God saves us, by which, that is, God gives us human access to salvation, is not laid out in a straight line. Some have light to which they respond while others don't. That appears to be true whether it is the light of the law or the light of nature. But the best light of all seems to be the gospel of Jesus. Having said that, and given the statements of the sufficiency of, but not the necessity of, belief/calling on the name of Jesus for salvation, it is hard to see how preaching should be interpreted except as giving more information rather than providing an exclusive means of human access to the work of Jesus.

Chapter 5

Toward an Expansive Gospel

I've presented some reasons to think that the image of God in us is not merely a set of universally shared features but is unique in each and every one of us. I've also presented both an existential challenge to exclusivism and a theoretical challenge to a narrowly construed inclusivism. I turn in this chapter to raise some questions about the metaphysical realism and ontological monism that underpins both CSE and CSI. That is, I move to include not merely the access component in the discussion but also the ontological basis for salvation—the work of Christ in the incarnation. I provide a metaphysically irrealist, ontological pluralist account of how salvation could be understood. I propose that God and the world, including the salvific realities provided by God, are themselves plural ways. The plural ways the world is give rise to conflicting but true accounts. There is, in short, *more than one means of accessing salvation through the work of Christ, both on the access level and on the ontological level.*

Section I presents a very brief overview of the background to what I call "theistic irrealism." Section II presents a general argument against metaphysical realism. The application to the salvific context is found in section III. Section IV explores a positive account of Christian salvific expansivism. Section V takes up various critical notes and questions and replies to them, thus further explaining expansivism.

Image, Incarnation, and Expansivism

I

I begin with a very brief summary of the key concepts and distinctions needed to grasp the irrealistic approach to ontology I take in the remainder of the chapter. For those who are truly interested in the technical philosophical accounts on which theistic irrealism is built, there is an appendix for you to pursue. Note that while the appendix is loaded with technical details, it can be safely left aside without losing the main points I wish to suggest.

Let's begin with concepts. We have a concept if we know how to use it. Some concepts are more basic than others, however. By "conceptual scheme" (or "conceptual framework") I have in mind the following: A conceptual scheme includes concepts the understanding of which are presupposed in employing a large number of our other, more specific concepts. Those concepts are highly general and thus many other concepts fall under them while they do not fall under other concepts. Such concepts are often irreducible and play important roles within our conceptual scheme—call them "basic concepts." A concept will not be basic unless it matters to a person in the sense that going through life without the concept would limit and reshape the person's conceptual life in significant ways.[1] Our conceptual schemes are part and parcel with our larger worldviews.

Our conceptual frameworks are historically situated and rooted. We do not all share the same conceptual schemes and that is to be celebrated and not ignored, as I believe many Christian accounts of salvation do. That we have different conceptual schemes, in turn, makes the world the many ways it is. I want to be clear here. By "many ways it is" I mean that we not only understand the world via an epistemologically plural framework but that *the world itself is ontologically plural*. The world actually is *many* ways, rather than a *monistic* way. If a monistic view of the world says that there is only one true description of the world, then a plural view of the world says there are many true (and competing or even contradictory) descriptions of the world. Hence, what is true is significantly and substantially relative to the conceptual scheme in which it is rooted and there are, therefore, truths that conflict with one another logically across conceptual schemes, even truths about Christian salvation. In short, the role of human noetic work in shaping the world extends both to human access to the salvation provided

---

1. I borrow heavily from Peter Strawson and Michael Lynch here.

by Christ and all the way to the incarnation of God and the various salvific means by which Jesus' life and work provide for our salvation.

But I want to add that just because conceptual schemes generate truths that are plural across schemes, it does not follow that the schemes are incommensurate or that just anything will go. I'm not, in short, arguing for a radical sort of relativism where Christianity is true in some scheme and not in another. From within the Christian account of the world, a good case can be made that there are thin concepts that are universally shared when those concepts are thickened out in competing ways, generating true, but contradictory, propositions about, let's say, Jesus or God or salvation and so forth.

The plural account of the Christian faith itself is likely to seem a radical claim for some traditional Christian ears, so I want to be clear, if perhaps a little redundant. This essay does *not* argue for some sort of religious pluralism where all the religions are equally true or where religious claims are mythically true and merely point to some reality beyond the myths. I am a Christian and, so far as I can tell, an orthodox one. I hold that the Christian Scriptures and the creeds present the fundamental truth about the world and God's creation of and love for the world.

Having described the notion of a conceptual scheme, here are some further basics. There is a coherent logic of relativism (or pluralism, as I prefer) that applies to pluralistic truth claims. Just as it is false to say that everything is possible while it is true to say that everything true is possibly true, so it is false to say that everything is relative while it is true to say that everything true is relatively true. Something's being true, in fact, guarantees that is possibly true. The logic works out perfectly well. Could it be that something's being true guarantees that is it also relatively true? I think so. The key here, however, is to recognize that some propositions are true relative to every conceptual scheme—what Lynch calls "virtual absolutes." These truths are relative to each conceptual scheme, but true in all conceptual schemes.

Concepts, furthermore, are embedded in conceptual schemes, but concepts are not static and fixed. Concepts can be understood in a crystalline or in a fluid way. Taking up a fluid understanding allows us to think of thick and thin properties. While on the thin level of properties, people might very well agree. As we thicken up properties, however, we will get quite different, even conflicting accounts of things. We can distinguish between minimal and robust concepts. A minimal concept of a thing—call it "F"—floats free of (most) metaphysical questions surrounding Fs. So a minimal concept is a way of thinking about something neutrally regarding its ontological nature. A robust concept of F, in contrast, is a concept whose ordinary use consists of a commitment to some particular ontological view of Fs. By engaging a worldview in which we have more than minimal concepts, we live in a world where our creative minds contribute to the conceptual schemes within which we live and hence the world is plural ways.

On the issue of truth, we can note that it is a property of propositions that can be minimally understood. Hence truth is a real property attaching to propositions; truth does not sink into the morass of epistemological accounts of truth. A proposition "p" is true, minimally, when and only when p is the case. What else might be required to give a fuller account of truth will depend on thickening up the concept of truth into, for example, a more robust form of the correspondence theory or some alternative.

Finally for this brief summary, pluralism can be expanded beyond the realm of truth. There may be, as Nelson Goodman had it, many worlds—worlds of metaphor, worlds of poetry, worlds of painting, and worlds of science. Not all these "ways the world is" are directly concerned with truth, but all are concerned with "rightness of rendering." The ways the world is cannot be made just any old way but must be made within the confines of the sort of thing one is creating. So there are clear limits on the way an ontology can be constructed, just as there are clear limits on how a chair can be constructed.

II

Let's turn directly to the metaphysical realism assumed in the background of CSE. In particular I note the tendency to claim that what is is not influenced by our epistemic or, more generally, our noetic contributions. The hinge-point can be summarized in a mantra: epistemology is not metaphysics! The following is a general argument against metaphysical realisms of the sort that claim there is (basically) only one true description of the universe and that in all but harmless and obvious sorts of ways (such as when my having an idea makes it the case that I'm having an idea) human noetic machinations do not make the world the way it is. After stating the general case against metaphysical realism, I apply it directly to conflicting views about how humans should access the work of Christ and eventually to the nature of Christ's work itself.

The overall position has several components, but the basic idea is not difficult to state. First, take many of the long-standing and seemingly intractable conflicts on various ontological issues and state the positions clearly as premises. Here it is important, but typically not difficult, to state the premises so that there is an actual contradiction between them. Add the law of noncontradiction as a premise. Now if one sticks to the metaphysical realist's commitment that human noetic work does not make the world the way it is, one can derive the conclusion that either metaphysical realism commits us to a deep skepticism (and we really can't do metaphysics except as guesswork) or there is more than one noetic structure each of which contains true statements that are contradictory to each other across structures. Supposing we should reject the skepticism, we are moved to irrealism. Irrealism, however, faces a number of challenges. I can't rehearse those at present but I refer the reader on to my other work.[2] One central issue that must be at least briefly discussed here, however, is that the irrealism I propose requires the existence of God. This God is not merely "made up" by human thought but is a God who is omniscient, omnipresent, omnipotent, loving, and freely creative. The reason for the presence of God in an irrealism in which human noetic work shapes nearly everything is not far to seek. God is needed to stop the sorts of pernicious regresses found in antirealistic theories. Once again, I refer the interested reader to my longer discussion of this view.[3]

With that brief introduction, here's the general argument for irrealism set out a little more formally.

A. It is impossible that both p and $-p$ be true (in the same conceptual scheme).

B. If p and $-p$ are both true, then there is more than one conceptual scheme such that p is true in one and $-p$ in another.

C. It is possible that both p and $-p$ are true.

D. p.

---

2. See McLeod-Harrison, *Make/Believing the World(s)*.

3. See McLeod-Harrison, "God and (Nearly) Global"; "The Many Ways God Is" and for the full-length treatment, *Make/Believing the World(s)*.

E. $-p$.

F. Therefore both p and $-p$ are true.

G. Therefore, there is more than one conceptual scheme such that p is true in one and $-p$ true in another.

H. Therefore, what is true is conceptual-scheme relative.

The move from C to D and E will appear to be the questionable one. It is at that juncture that we must be very clear and careful. We cannot introduce any epistemic or noetic valuing of the various premises in the argument. *To do so is to already grant that metaphysical claims are not independent of noetic work.* In particular, it is tempting to reject F because we "know" that either D or E is false. But that already assumes a realist interpretation of the law of noncontradiction and we have another place where we already grant that metaphysical claims are not independent of noetic work. But the metaphysical realist has insisted that we not sneak epistemic or noetic contributions into any of our metaphysical claims. So unless we want to move to the position that we simply never can know (or even rationally believe) a metaphysical proposition, the scales are tipped toward some sort of irrealism. Humans actually do contribute to the nature of reality.

Let's flesh out the argument. Consider the following supporting argument.

1. Either our conceptualizing-epistemizing premises A, D, and E contributes to A, D, and E being the case or it does not. (Alternatively, we might say: our conceptualizing the world makes A and D the case or A and E the case, but not both.)

2. If our conceptualizing-epistemizing A, D, and E contributes to A, D, and E being the case, then irrealism obtains. (Alternatively: if our conceptualizing the world makes either A and D the case or A and E the case, but not both, then irrealism obtains.)

3. If our conceptualizing-epistemizing A, D, and E does not contribute to A, D, and E being the case, then the irrealist argument is successful, and irrealism obtains. (Alternatively: if our conceptualizing the world does not make either A and D the case or A and E the case, but not both, then the irrealist argument is successful and irrealism obtains.)

4. Therefore, irrealism obtains.

Toward an Expansive Gospel

Some explanation is in order.

Taken straight forwardly, premise 2 simply gives us irrealism. Suppose we epistemize A, D, and E according to one conceptual framework rather than another. That is, suppose that we conceptualize the world such that either D or E turns out to be true. The antecedent of 2 then is either true or false. If it is true, then the truth of A, D, and E depends somehow on our conceptualizing-epistemizing them, which in turn rests on our conceptualizing the world one way rather than another, in which case there is surely more than one way the world is and no reason apart from our conceptualizing the world to pick one over the other, for there is more than one way to conceptualize-epistemize A, D, and E. What is true thus is conceptual-scheme relative. Irrealism obtains. On the other hand, if the antecedent of 2 is false, then the truth of A, D, and E has nothing to do with conceptualizing-epistemizing and thus conceptualizing-epistemizing is irrelevant to the irrealist argument presented above. This irrelevance drives a large wedge between epistemology and metaphysics, precisely what the realist typically claims. Thus 3 comes into play.

The antecedent of 3 says that the truth of A, D, and E is in no way shaped by our conceptualizing-epistemic stance toward A, D, and E. So, if we do not in any way conceptualize-epistemize the premises in the irrealist argument, then we cannot appeal to reasons to reject any of the premises. That leaves three possibilities with regard to the truth or falsity of A, D, and E. However, before exploring those possibilities, it is important to note that the discussion is not focused on defending the truth of A, D, and E (that would be to rank them epistemically), but rather on understanding what actual epistemic neutrality looks like in regard to this argument. So the issue isn't whether we have evidence for or against the truth of any of the premises. If we had such evidence, it would be because we had already conceptualized the world one way rather than another. We must first have a conceptualized world in order to have reasons. The real question is, since we aren't allowed to appeal to such evidence, how we are to treat A, D, and E? As it turns out, it looks like the position that claims all the premises are true is at least as viable as any other position—in fact, superior to some—and therefore the argument goes through.

Let's consider the possible combination of truth values for the premises. First, let's suppose all the premises are false. No solace for realism is found here. Because all three are false, A is false. But then contradictions would be possible and that is a fate worse than irrealism, for then anything goes. We are left with what we might call a true and complete antirealism that is no better than an unconstrained extreme relativism. So if we get irrealism if A, D, and E are true, we get a radical kind of antirealism if A is false. Taking this route won't help the realist. The second possibility is that some of A, D, and E are true and others false. But which? We can tell right away that it won't be A that is false, without rendering the worlds not only multiple but completely relative. That leaves us with D and E. While it is possible that one is true and the other not, without introducing some reason to pick one over another (which, by assumption, we cannot do, for that is to epistemize them, that is, to have already conceptualized the world) we look to be on shaky ground. Why should we take the situation one way rather than another? According to the realist dichotomy between epistemology and ontology, believing, knowing, taking, accepting, and so forth, have nothing to do (generally) with the way reality is. In remaining epistemically neutral, we cannot, by supposition, epistemically rank-order the premises one way or another. That leaves the third possibility, that A, D, and E are all true. But then F, G, and H follow, and irrealism obtains. One could suggest that evidence can be marshaled against A, D, and E. But to marshal such evidence is to epistemize the premises, for we will have already conceptualized the world one way rather than another. Again, we can't do that, by supposition. Hence, if we are consistent in not introducing epistemic rank-ordering, the irrealist argument is successful, and irrealism obtains.

Now a particularly recalcitrant realist may still say that the world is the way it is completely independent of the way we relate to it epistemically. In particular, he may admit how my discussion of the first and third possible combinations of truth values go, but not admit the second. Why not just retreat to the position that we don't know which of D and E is false, but that one must be true while the other is false? There is no need to introduce epistemic rankings, you need only admit that one isn't true. The irrealist response to this is simple and direct. The realist must admit that realism is stuck, on the one hand, between the rock of admitting that conceptualizing-epistemizing contributes to the metaphysical nature of the world, and hence what turns out to be true or not, and, on the other hand, the hard place of skepticism. But actually the irrealist can press another issue here, pushing the realist into an even worse position. As it turns out, there is no noncircular way of being a realist, once the realist retreats to the position of admitting that realism could be wrong about the way the world is.

Premise A is actually metaphysically neutral between there being a singular world and multiple worlds. That is, although A is taken to be true, there is no built-in commitment to a singular-world realist interpretation of the law of noncontradiction over against an irrealist interpretation. An irrealist not only can desire to hold onto A but is certainly free to as well. One difference between the realist and the irrealist on this score is that the irrealist can truly remain open to where the argument might go. The irrealist who remains epistemically neutral about A, D, and E actually doesn't beg any epistemic questions about them. By remaining neutral in this way, the irrealist gets the conclusions, F, G, and H. About this, the irrealist is quite sanguine.

How can the realist avoid these irrealist conclusions? What reason can the realist proffer to defend the single-world interpretation of A? None, except, perhaps, to assert that there is only one way the world is along with the singular-world realist interpretation of the law of noncontradiction. But that is the realist thesis itself and that begs the question against the irrealist position. Realism is not the default position on these matters. Irrealism is on ground just as solid. In fact, irrealism is, I submit, on better ground.

The realist might say, in a final attempt to defend realism, that on the grounds of the irrealist argument, circular reasoning is acceptable. We know that a proposition follows from itself, if we stick to logic; "p therefore p" is perfectly valid, deductively. "Realism is true" follows from "realism is true." So what's wrong with begging the question against the irrealist position? The irrealist retort is simple: Go ahead, but that appeal to logic stripped of epistemology proves the irrealist point and doesn't help the realist at all. There are many odd things about deductive logic, stripped of all epistemic concerns. One of them is that logic alone cannot tell us anything about the world. Logic is at best neutral vis-à-vis these matters. The irrealist does not end up in the same skeptical boat because at least the irrealist has provided an argument. The irrealist provides A, D, and E. And it looks like one can substitute whatever one wishes for p and –p. Perhaps one can substitute that humans have rights based in our natures and that humans do not have rights based in our natures. Or perhaps that abortion is acceptable and abortion is not acceptable. And so on. (There are important limitations on what can be used here, but this isn't the place to explore them.)[4]

4. See McLeod-Harrison, *Make/Believing the World(s)*.

Image, Incarnation, and Expansivism

Pick your favorite metaphysical issue and take from it two contradictory claims. All the irrealist needs is some argument with contradictory statements substituted for p and –p. She need not offer those as epistemically ranked propositions. She need only offer the bare logic of the situation. She needs no other reason. The strict separation of epistemic concerns from metaphysical ones opens the door to irrealism, just the opposite result from what a typical realist might suspect.

One might have further questions about the first premise of the argument. One might, for example, worry that it "front loads" an ontological pluralism in from the beginning.[5] There are certainly issues about the status of the law of noncontradiction on which premise 1 rests. I can't settle those here. In fact, I'm not aware of anyone who has made a very good case as to why the law is so central to the way the world is or the way we think about the world. We all just take it to be the case. I propose as one plausible way to think about the law is that it has a dual, metaphysical/epistemological basis in the mind of God. So, the law is what it is because God's thoughts ultimately make it so. God's making it so, however, need not commit one to some sort of Cartesian relativity on the matter. God's very thoughts and God's very nature may be so closely aligned that the law is fixed. Once it is set into place, however, it applies within each and every conceptual scheme or it simply applies to the world (on a realist account of the world).

In short, the argument does not let irrealism get off the ground because it is premised on a kind of perspectivalism, e.g., p and –p only mean what they mean because they are properties of a conceptual scheme vs. assessed as "mind-independent facts."[6] One can simply drop the parenthetical clause from premise 1, remaining neutral on the status of the law of noncontradiction. As I noted above, if it did turn out that the law somehow didn't hold, we would all be committed to the most radical of ontological pluralisms, a sort of total relativism about what is true. That would not be irrealism as I think of it but a totalizing or global anti-realism. Instead, I suggest, what is true is true because of the way the various conceptual schemes make the world, but one can get to that view without boot-strapping oneself into it. Once you've got truth, you've always got the law of non-contradiction in play.

---

5. One of the journal reviewers made a comment to this effect. Besides these brief comments here, I've dealt with the issue at length in *Make/Believing the World(s)*.

6. This is a paraphrase of the reviewer's comments.

So, the overall view developed here does not commit us to the position that truth is dependent on the noetic contribution of humans. The concept of truth can be understood, following William Alston, as minimal and one can construct a realist, if minimalist, account of truth.[7] Nevertheless, what is dependent on human noetic work is the way the world is even though truth is not thus dependent. What makes "p" true is p. Such an account of truth is not epistemic or deflationary.[8] So even though various and substantial aspects of the world are made by human noetic work, what makes a proposition true is the way the world ends up being within the various conceptual schemes and not the conceptual or epistemic schemes themselves. Being true is a real property (and hence truth is not deflated) and it does not itself depend on human noetic contributions (and hence truth is not epistemic). The world itself, however, does depend on our noetic contributions.

III

With the general rejection of metaphysical realism laid out, here's an application of the first part of the above general argument drawing on two specific claims made about the nature of the human access to the salvific ontology.

I. It is impossible that both A *one has access to the salvific ontology by faith alone* and –A *one has access to the salvific ontology by works alone* be true (in a single conceptual scheme).

J. If A and –A are both true, then there is more than one conceptual scheme such that A is true in one and –A in another.

K. It is possible that both A and –A are true.

L. A.

M. –A.

N. Therefore both A and –A are true.

O. Therefore, there is more than one conceptual scheme such that A is true in one and –A true in another.

---

7. See Alston, *A Realist Conception*.
8. See footnote 12 on page 17.

Before moving ahead, it is helpful to note that the account of faith vs. works would need to be spelled out carefully in order to get an actual contradiction between L and M. Here is a quick attempt at that spelling out.

Often faith is thought of as including works. Faith without works is dead, says James. To be clear, however, let's say someone comes to faith on her deathbed and has no time to develop a working life of faith. Assuming that her faith is not, in fact, a type of work, such a person on A has what it takes to access the work of Jesus Christ in terms of salvation, and she will be in the proper salvific relationship with God. Had she lived, of course, she might very well have developed a working life of faith. But theologically, her faith is *expressed* by her works. Her works are not (by themselves, let's say) enough for (or in some sense, even relevant to) her salvation. Faith is needed and is, so far forth, enough. But in the contradictory statement (works alone gives one access to salvation) the person believes that her works are the means of access to God's provision of salvation. Such a one thinks God asks of her to be a good person, to love her neighbor, and so forth. While she believes in God, her belief is an intellectual assent rather than a fiduciary relationship of trust. If asked, she would say she will enter heaven not because of her belief but because God will judge how well she lived. Her actions show, she might say, that she tried to live as Christ wants her to live and that grants her access to the salvific framework provided by Jesus. (We might even say, theologically, that her work is *expressed* by her faith, just the reverse to the faith-alone person described above.)

Now, it seems, A and –A are actually contradictory. If that doesn't satisfy the reader, one can just replace my suggestions with an explicit contradiction. For example, A could be "saved by faith alone" while –A is "saved by something other than faith alone."

To return to the argument itself, I remind the reader that the move from K to L and M must be carefully considered so as to introduce no epistemic valuation. If such valuation is introduced, irrealism is already admitted. But if one is careful, then what is true will be shown to be relative to conceptual schemes. Nevertheless, even with this caution, the argument's conclusion will perhaps still be met with skepticism by the hard-core metaphysical realist and likely met with an even more strident skepticism by many Christians. I believe such skepticism is often more existential than strictly rational or evidential, and I would encourage the reader to look beyond her or his immediate intuitive response to see the good that can come out of understanding reality in the irrealist way being suggested before simply rejecting (or perhaps worse, ignoring) the argument.

IV

Here I turn to a positive account of expansivism in order to persuade the reader further. Where does the argument above leave us? One direction would be to take such theological claims as A and −A to be completely antirealist in nature so that their ontological status is entirely brought about by humans epistemically or conceptually. I reject this approach for a number of reasons. First, the resulting antirealism simply puts too much power in the hands—or more circumspectly, the minds—of humans. We don't make things up whole-cloth as some more radical antirealists seem to suggest. Second, such a view makes nonsense out of much of the Christian tradition. As William Alston notes, we are loved by God and it would be odd to think that we are loved by nothing more than a figment of our conceptual schemes.[9] Third, it would be strange, indeed, that humans create the very thing worthy of worship. But the radical antirealist approach is not the only route that can be taken, nor the best one for traditional Christians. There is, instead, another road. The basic idea is that God *at the divine core* is not dependent upon human conceptual or epistemic schemes, but insofar as humans interact with the divine, God is shaped by our noetic contributions.

How might that work? Human conceptual schemes can shape how God is vis-à-vis human interaction, *but not at the divine core* because there are thin properties shared across all conceptual schemes (what have been called "virtual absolutes") and those are each thickened up via human noetic work in each conceptual scheme.[10] The thin properties describe God's core. For example, we might say, thinly, that God is omnipresent, omniscient, omnipotent, omnibenevolent, and creator. These properties can truly be predicated of God no matter in which conceptual scheme they are framed. However, there is not much meat on those bones. God and the thin properties must be thickened up in a (human) conceptual scheme. While everyone may agree that God is omnipotent (let's say, being able to do whatever is logically possible) there are many theories and ways people

---

9. Alston, "Realism."

10. The basic idea of thin vs. thick properties as a means of help explain ontological pluralism is borrowed from Michael Lynch, as is the notion of virtual absolutes. See his *Truth in Context*.

think about what that comes to. It is at the level of theory and thinking that God's properties get thickened up into the way God is in a given conceptual scheme.

Here one must talk about a certain sort of eschatological component to theistic irrealism, for many proposed conceptual schemes attempt to exclude God. Such exclusions are, it could be suggested, wallpapering schemes where God is ignored. Yet since God is the creator, God cannot, in the end, be ignored metaphysically for God is needed as the underpinning of human creative work. The main point here, and in terms of Christian orthodoxy, is that God exists and exists across and in all (well-formed) conceptual schemes. No human conceptualizing will change God at this core level.

But at the thick level, God is different across conceptual schemes. The thick properties describe how God is, so to speak, *logically after* interaction with human conceptual schemes. On the level of thick properties what turns out to be true in one conceptual scheme is contradictory to what is true in other conceptual schemes. How God's omnipotence is in one conceptual scheme is not the same and, in fact, can be quite contradictory to, how it is in another conceptual scheme. And so with omniscience, omnipresence, omnibenevolence, and creativity.

Of course, there is more to the Christian God than the properties just discussed. To get something a little fuller in front of us, consider the Nicene Creed as a basic thin description of God and the divine relationship to the world. Of course, the Nicene Creed is full of metaphor as well as literal description of God, but a fully detailed account of theistic irrealism will have to allow for metaphorical truths just as all good Christian theology must. Setting that issue aside for now, the main point I want to make is that the various claims of the Creed can rest on thin properties that are filled out more thickly according to the many ways of understanding the Creed. There are limits, here, of course. But the central issue for our purposes is that all the claims about God becoming incarnate in the historical Jesus, and his life, death, and resurrection, can be thinly understood as true in all conceptual schemes, but thickly true in some conceptual schemes but not others.

Let's apply these general suggestions more specifically to the question of salvation. Let's say Mary holds −A while Joseph holds A. On these suppositions, it is true in one conceptual scheme that God saves Mary by the work of Christ while she accesses salvation by works alone. It is true in another conceptual scheme that God saves Joseph by the work of Christ while he accesses salvation through faith alone. More specifically it is true in Mary's conceptual scheme that the path to Christ is through works alone. It is true in Joseph's conceptual scheme that the path to Christ is through faith alone. The difference is how each individual Christian (or more likely, her larger socially, theologically, and conceptually connected set of Christian compatriots) conceptualizes her access to the salvific relationship with Christ. The result is an inclusivist account of salvation's access with an exclusive ontological base in the incarnation, life, and work of Jesus Christ. If the thin description of access to Christ's work were "come follow me," the thicker descriptions could include what that looks like right down to the individual's specific needs. The rich young ruler needed to give up his goods to follow Jesus, Nicodemus to be born again,[11] the woman at the well to broaden her theology and conception of God, Peter to overcome his wide emotional swings, Paul his hardened, pharisaical ways, Martha her ties to the kitchen, and the "Canaanite" woman to engage Jesus in a theological argument. Of course, in each case there is more to the access to Jesus' work, but each of us comes into relationship with Christ with our own thoughts, fears, needs, and conceptions of Jesus and his work. Some of these folk engaged Jesus before his work on earth was over. Some only after, and some both. But in each case, the ontological grounding of salvation (the total work of Christ) comes into play for the individual human in and through their own thoughts, beliefs, attitudes, and so forth; that is, through their conceptual schemes.

But it is not just human *access* that is shaped by our circumstances and hence our conceptual schemes, but *the work of Jesus himself*. For example, perhaps the various accounts of the atonement are all true, in their respective conceptual schemes. So the substitutionary, the moral, and the ransom accounts are all accurate—just true in different conceptual schemes. If such is the case, it does not deny the virtual fact of Christ's work on the cross. There is a thin account of Christ's death and resurrection that holds in all

---

11. Jesus does say that no one could see the kingdom unless she or he is born from above or born again. So it could be that this metaphor (being born) could replace the "come follow me" noted in the text. But the central point I want to make is not that I have exactly the right metaphor to use to describe the appropriate relationship to Christ but rather that those fundamental metaphors—following or being born again—are made specific by Christ for each individual. Nicodemus is upbraided by Jesus for taking Jesus too literally. Nicodemus seems to be blinded by his status as a teacher of Israel rather than freed by it and Jesus is pointing the way through his particular blindness.

well-formed conceptual schemes, given in summary form in the Nicene Creed. Thus, there is a sort of exclusivism involved in the claims of Christianity. It is an exclusivism of the thin reality of God as present and active via the incarnation and the subsequent presence of the Holy Spirit. But all the competing claims in thick accounts are true (assuming that each conceptual scheme generates a coherent, complete account). The thick accounts are just not true in every conceptual scheme. Thus, there is an objectivity, if one wants a label, to the presence and reality of God and God's salvific work. But there is also a broad range of competing and yet fully true ways God is in the world. The salvific work of Christ is actual, but irrealistically so, rooted both in the conceptual work of human persons and the mysterious reality who is the God of Christian worship and belief.

Returning to the three components of CSE from chapter 1, I'm suggesting that 3—the Christian exclusivist access component—is false. There are *many* means of accessing the work of Christ mentioned in 2—the ontologically monist component. Each of these ways—even when they appear to contradict one another—are true (or could be, if complete, coherent, etc.) because what is true is relative to the conceptual scheme in which it is embedded. Furthermore, even how we understand 2 can be broadly construed and each of the ways it is construed—even where they appear to contradict one another—are true because of the conceptual scheme in which they are embedded. That is, the world and its salvific framework are themselves different in different conceptual schemes. Finally, the various true versions of the means of accessing salvation may be coordinated logically (in some instances, at least) with the various true versions of the nature of salvation, the nature of sin, the atonement, and even the nature of Christ across various conceptual schemes. The differences occur on the thick level, whereas on the thin level, the description is universal across all conceptual schemes.

Even if all this is correct, however, nothing has been done to explain how those apparently outside the Christian tradition can access the work of Christ for salvation. My account does not limit access to the work of Christ to Christians per se. It may turn out that those who are un-, ill-, or misinformed of the work of Christ can still access the salvific work of Christ. Perhaps even those who make a well-informed and free decision to reject Christ (say because of some deep harm done by the church) are not self-condemned, but could be saved by the work of Christ via some apparently non-Christian means of access to that gracious work of God's.

At this point one might suggest that no matter how much one's conceptual scheme is stretched, it must ultimately include some connection to what I've called the "thin" account of God, the work of Christ, and the power of the Holy Spirit. A Buddhist, no matter how sincere, is simply not relying of the work of Christ. But here we can introduce a parallel to the referential account suggested by Alston and noted above. The Buddhist might very well be referring to the work of Christ even though systematically misdescribing the source of her salvation. Here too we might recall the very important eschatological aspects of theistic irrealism referred to briefly earlier. The atheist, whether Buddhist or Western post-Enlightenment, may very well be referring to God's salvific work in her or his life and thereby be saved. Humanity looks on the stature of a person whereas God looks at the heart, as the Scriptures report. There is so much more to an actual Christ-like life than believing or saying "the right things," so we seem on shaky ground indeed to rule out the possibility that God's grace might work in cases outside the Christian faith itself.

It is worth mentioning as well that the modified direct reference approach just noted would open doors, perhaps, to a richer, more serious, approach to inter-religious dialogue. Often religious dialogue for traditional Christians turns out to be a tool to show where other religions are false. We want to turn it into a real dialogue from which one can learn how to think Christianly about various matters. We also want to remain committed to the core account of the Christian faith. This is possible on theistic irrealism while also remaining open to not only hear but perhaps to appropriate various descriptions of God from other religious perspectives. This general point is true not only of God but of various other broadly theological issues as well—anthropology, perhaps, or the nature of sin. There may be a good many conceptual understandings and tools found in non-Christian religions that would help Christians develop better and fuller conceptual approaches to the way God is. I fear we (traditional) Christians often time miss such insights for fear of "getting things wrong" according to our own tradition. With theistic irrealism and an openness to inclusivism vis-à-vis human access to salvation, we might be able to take our neighbors more seriously as people who are saved but who have insights we don't have.

Image, Incarnation, and Expansivism

V

This section contains various critical notes and questions and my responses to them. First, a critic might suggest that there is no reason to think Christianity is the only true religion. Why not take a similar approach from the point of view of Buddhism or Islam, claiming that there is a thin version of one or the other of these religions that can be thickened up in various ways and that the (Buddhist or Muslim) thin version provides the ultimate ontological basis for salvation via a sort of direct reference? In response, I admit that nothing developed here or elsewhere shows that Christianity is the true religion. In other places, I've tried to show that theistic irrealism and the concomitant ontological pluralism is consistent with orthodox Christianity. There is nothing, so far forth, to show that only Christianity can support theistic irrealism. Indeed, Islam and Judaism, along with other theistic religious traditions, might work as well. However, the nontheistic religions will not, I believe. The reason, in brief, is that theistic irrealism requires a mind such as God's to provide for necessities and to stop the pernicious regresses mentioned in chapter 1. Again, I refer the reader to my other work on this matter. However, I would add that theistic irrealism is open to the possibility of a number of apologetic approaches to the various religions to seek to discover which of the many, if any, is the true one. That project should be encouraged so long as it is taken up in the mode and spirit of open dialogue rather than closed judgment. The same approach as one might take with metaphysical realism can be taken within theistic irrealism.

My irrealistic proposal has one advantage over realism, however. Ecumenical approaches to doctrine in general often seem to strip down the content of the Christian believer's commitments to a bare bones approach. With the additional (and legitimate) concerns of those outside the Christian faith that their doctrinal voices be heard, appreciated, and not rejected out of hand, ecumenism sometimes moves to more or less empty Christian propositions of their "literal" meaning and/or their claim to truth. Such striping down, I suggest, leaves one at best with a sort of salvific religious pluralism rather than something peculiarly Christian. One who holds to Christian salvific expansivism does not need to move to salvific religious pluralism.

I'd like to respond also to a number of questions posed by various reviewers.[12] Is the view presented here really a panentheistic irrealism rather than a theistic irrealism? That is, indeed, a good question. After Philip Clayton (as hearty a panentheist as any) read *Make/Believing the World(s)*, the book on which the work in this chapter and the appendix is based, he wondered the same thing. I think there are clearly some affinities. I don't believe in the end, however, that this view is panentheistic, although I think one way in which God *might be* is panentheistic. God in panentheism seems, however, to emerge (more of less entirely) out of the natural order, a view I would reject, at least so far as I can tell based on reading panentheistic work. Perhaps there is an "antecedent" way God is that is influenced by the "consequent" level because of the way the natural order is. That mirrors in some ways what I've said. But even with that, there is nothing in panentheism *per se* that involves human conceptualizing making God one way rather than another. That is, there is no clear pluralism in, for example, Clayton's work. Could the model of God's omniscience that attends panentheism be one of the ways God's omniscience is (in one of the human conceptual schemes)? Yes, I think so.

A host of further questions could be asked here. How does one know whether one is developing an adequate thickly true understanding of God within some conceptual scheme given the pluralism of irrealism? Why should one thicken-up? What's the motivation? What does it really accomplish given what thinly understood conceptions already accomplish? If one doesn't know whether one is developing an adequate thickly true understanding of God, doesn't that create a lot of existential anxiety in terms of whether one is getting it "right"?

Let's take these in order. First, how does one know whether one is developing an adequate thickly true understanding of God within some conceptual scheme given the pluralism of irrealism? Here it is helpful to know that the "rightness" of our theory and ontology building is rooted in at least three things: God, God's communication to us, and our own reasoned, emotional, human responses. Like all theory building, one takes the data one has and tries to explain it in the most cogent and complete way possible. Of course, many Christians don't spend their time working on theology, although most of us do spend some of our time on that project, which includes the way we live out our lives. While one can never be completely

---

12. Many of the questions listed here came in response to a version of this chapter first sent to *Philosophia Christi*. I thank the reviewer for the questions.

sure one is "getting it right," it is important to remember the fact that one of the primary modes of being in God's image is the creative mode. Adam's earliest tasks included naming the animals, and the primary (though not the only) thing we learn about God in the Genesis account is that God is immensely creative. The creative image of God in Adam included not just naming the animals but creating the whole new category of "livestock." That could be taken as the creation of new ontological categories via a conceptual scheme. But the main point is that we need to continue working on our creations to make them the best they can be. This, of course, is all done in history and within the inherited accounts of God we have from Scripture and tradition—even from our parents and immediate peers. One doesn't thicken God up out of whole cloth. It comes cut and shaped before we get started. There will be false starts, places where we have to sew the cloth again, patch, and so forth. The actual criteria for getting things right are manifold, but include coherence, faithfulness to the past, faithfulness to Scripture, faithfulness to the social community in which we live, whether the account sheds light on various bits of data, creative insights that expand the greatness of God, and so on. Of course, like in all accounts of theorizing, the theorizing is never complete, but historical. The theories are always developing and expanding. But in the end, we can never "get outside" the theory to check it against "reality." We are making reality by the theorizing. On theistic irrealism large aspects of reality are generated out of our conceptual schemes and thus we are, in some respects, closer to reality on this view and there is, therefore, less room for skepticism than on realism.

The next three questions are linked. Why should one thicken-up? What is the motivation? What does it really accomplish given what thinly understood conceptions already accomplish? There is a misunderstanding, perhaps, in these questions. First, one has no choice but to thicken up the thin concepts. Take a non-theological example. Suppose a number of philosophers are talking about a concept, say death. The thin concept might be captured by the notion "cessation of life." All the philosophers will agree to that thin notion. But it doesn't do much work in, let's say, accounts of the meaningfulness of death. Each of the philosophers might take the thin concept in very different directions. One might think cessation of life comes to brain cessation, another to heart cessation, another to separation of soul from body, and another, spiritual cessation (the end of the soul rather than the body). These thickened notions of death play a role in the conceptual scheme of each philosopher that the thinner notion simply won't capture.

The philosophers have to thicken out the concept in order for the theoretical work (and indeed, the ontological work) to be done. So it is with God's thin properties. There are a variety of ways of thickening up the notion of omnipotence—along, let's say, Whiteheadian/Hartshornian lines, along traditional perfect being theological lines, along open theistic lines, and so forth. While the basic notion of omnipotence (can do anything logically possible) would be agreed to by all the philosophers (let's say), what it comes to when thickened up will be quite different in various conceptual schemes and hence God's omnipotence will be different in each of these schemes.

As to motivation and what is actually accomplished, the answers are fairly short, given what has been suggested. First, the motivation is just that we are making ways the world is because it is a God-placed creativity within us. We have a propensity to create because God is creative and we are God's image. Second, what is accomplished is just a making of the way the world is, God is, we are, etc. But all of this is descriptive of *what* we do, not so much of *why* we do it. So in this sense, these last three questions seem somewhat misguided.

Finally, if one doesn't know whether one is developing an adequate thickly true understanding of God, doesn't that create a lot of existential worry about whether one is getting it "right"? This is an important question. Earlier I developed the argument noting an existential reason to reject realism, viz., that there is the possibility of an existential crisis of faith that develops in one's spiritual life—a worry that one has gotten it wrong. But does the irrealistic account fare any better on the existential question? In reply one can observe that the difference is between realism and irrealism in the salvific context is that someone who is deeply committed to CSE may be concerned much more about "getting it right" because there are so many ways to go wrong. The irrealist, in contrast, can relax, knowing first that she is "on the way" to a right rendering of the world and that there are, in fact, multiple ways of creating an appropriate way the world is. Since I think irrealism is best paired with inclusivism about salvation rather than exclusivism, once again, existentially it seems a holder of expansivism is more likely to relax.

Does theistic irrealism commit one to open theism? Once again, I don't think so, although the open theistic account of God seems to be one of the ways God is. However, there is an eschatological component to theistic irrealism. Not any account of God will pass muster in the end.

Image, Incarnation, and Expansivism

There are limits to the ways in which we can "build" God. But those limits are not so narrow that there is only one way God is in the eschaton. We will all, so to speak, live in relationship with the God we have "made." But the God we will have made will not be made willy-nilly. God's core can never be wallpapered over, any more than God's existence can be. Those of us who construct an open God, insofar as that ontology pleases God, will live with that open God. Those of us who construct a Calvinist God, insofar as that ontology pleases God, will live with that Calvinist God. And so on. I reject the notion that God is static. Here I mean static in terms of the ways in which humans can construct God. God is dynamic on both perfect-being and open theology models, but at God's core, the divinity is neither, but open to both—not static in *that* sense. God fails to be static *in the divine core*. Insofar as one thinks God is entirely fixed and incapable of interacting with human conceptual schemes, one will be unhappy with the view developed here.

That someone is committed to the immutability of God does nothing to theistic irrealism. However, if such an absolute commitment were a blind and closed account of how God might be, then that would be contrary to irrealism. I propose that theistic irrealism gets at the underpinnings of our various conflicting ontologies—our ways of taking God—by making God various ways. Those conflicting ontologies, however, are not *competing* ontologies. That is, they are not competing in the sense that they are all trying to describe the monistic or singular way the world is. Instead, they are all true (at least they will be, in the eschaton) and hence not in competition with one another. One of the strengths of the proposed view is that we can spend our time discussing or explaining things rather than trying to win arguments. But those discussions or explanations are not ever finished here. Right now, while we toil away at our earthly tasks, our various ways of constructing God (and other things as well) are incomplete, short-sighted, sometimes vague, and so forth. We are, I believe, in the business of building ways the world is, not in the business of selling the final version of the real estate.

Finally, let me return to the sorts of concern noted by Alston about anti-realism as applied to God. His concerns come down to the observation that the notion of God on such views makes nonsense of God's (actual) love for us, God's (actually) being an object worthy of worship. It's hard to be loved by, or to worship, an entirely fictional creature of our imaginations. The God described in theistic irrealism is, however, no mere creature of our imaginations. Our relationship with God is fundamentally social in the understanding of theistic irrealism. We are social creatures of God's own making and God is fundamentally social at the divine core. God is a Trinity of persons, and we are invited into relationship with those three persons.

One way to think of how we shape God via our conceptual schemes is to think of how we shape, for example, our spouses. After long years spent together my spouse is changed by the ways in which I think of her. Most of our social relationships are like this. Our relationship with God even more so. But it is two-way street. Not only is my spouse changed by my ways of thinking, but I, too, am changed by my spouse's ways of thinking about me. So much more so with God. God's core is love and essentially so. God's interactions with us are meant to bring us into full and forever relationships with the divine love. God invites us to enter such relationships by God's graciously encouraging us to shape and mold God. God and the salvation God provides is of course rooted in the divine core of love, but love "is patient; love is kind; love is not envious or boastful or arrogant or rude. It does not insist on its own way; it is not irritable or resentful; it does not rejoice in wrongdoing, but rejoices in the truth. It bears all things, believes all things, hopes all things, endures all things." Perhaps God endures a lot of stretching to encourage us to be in a relationship with the divine self that we can grasp. Perhaps, indeed, theistic irrealism is the ultimate in incarnational theology. But the point, in the end, of incarnational theology is to help us along the road to being like God. In the give and take of marriage, we are to learn to love. In the give and take of divine relationship—not just at a spiritual-formation level, but a theoretical level as well—we are to learn to love. We are shaped, however, by God more than God is shaped by us. That doesn't entail, however, that God isn't shaped by us. Salvation, ultimately, is about us being shaped more fully into the image of God. That image, however, is at least partly dependent on us. But only partly. God's voice is heard in the eschaton. But rather than merely being a voice of judgment about how we have faulty beliefs about God, it will be a voice perhaps saying that God appreciates our efforts at shaping the divine self—but, says God, do you think it needs a little tweaking on this score? Not just anything will go in the theistic irrealistic eschaton. But probably more will go than is typically allowed on the metaphysically realist account to which traditional Christian theology is so often thought to be rooted. And all of this recognizes, of course, the deep historicity of the human person. God's salvation is not just

Image, Incarnation, and Expansivism

an abstract, one size fits all. It is personal, individual, and historical. That, in the end, is what Christ's incarnational provision of salvation is all about.

The image of God in us is both shared among all humans and also unique to each of us. This is no less true of Jesus than it is of the rest of us. Jesus' incarnation enables the fullness of God to enter into what it is to be human. This is no less important for God than it is for us. God's engaging the world in incarnate form makes him not only the image of God with all the divine attributes but also made in the image of God with all the human attributes (except for sin). Jesus's incarnation, however, is not a singular way. We are all historically situated. We understand and, if the argument of this chapter is correct, we shape and influence the very nature of God's incarnation among us. God has provided out of the love that is at the core of the divine being salvation from the many ills and weaknesses of being human. Salvation and our access to it is shaped by our needs, personalities, quirks, and historical situations. Jesus meets us in those needs, personalities, quirks, and historical situations.

God is at core a social being. Father, Son, and Holy Spirit have extended their love for one another to include us in the *perichoresis* that is the divine dance of love. God, in the Son, becomes our dance partner and he moves and shapes us as we move and shape him. That is part of what it is to be in the image of God. But here I'd like to side with the Orthodox view of distinguishing between the image and likeness of God. For the Orthodox, the likeness of God is our capacity to become "second gods" or "gods by grace." As we interact with the divine being, we are shaped and moved and molded into the kinds of beings we are meant to be. But that does not force us all into the same mold. We are as unique in the kingdom of heaven as Jesus is. But what he is by nature (the incarnate God) we become by grace (incarnate gods). That, in the end, is the point of salvation.

Should a last-minute critic suggest that my siding with the Orthodox on the matters just discussed undermines my whole pluralistic project, I have a reply. That is, this is my way of working things out, rooted in my history, my experience, and my existential situation. Others will provide alternatives. That is all to the good. So far as each of us engages God, engages the use of our conceptual schemes as they are rooted in our experiences and histories and, finally, so long as God, in the eschaton, approves of (or, perhaps better, is delighted by) our creative efforts to respond to the love of God, we will all be interacting with the God we have helped to shape and inside a salvation that is tailor-made for the unique persons we are.

Finally, the Pauline image of the church as the body of Christ should not be treated as a mere metaphor. Salvation is about saving the entirety of the human person and linking us forever into the Body of Christ. In the doctrine of the communion of the saints, as understood, at least, by the Roman Catholic Church, we all become so united that the pain of each is the pain of all and the good for one is the good for all. This can happen, I propose, only by us becoming so humble—humble to the point of death—that we cease holding on to ourselves and give our entire beings over to the one who came among us. He comes to save and to heal. As we approach him, think about him, rely on him, and love him, he will become what each of us needs him to be to provide salvation for us in our unique being. That is an expansive gospel.

Chapter 6

On Becoming Second Incarnations

Salvation, if the argument of this book is on the right path, turns out to be a particularized process, localized to the particular human I am, with the particular history I have. So it is with you and your particular history and so it is everyone and their particular histories. But we move into salvation because Jesus shows us the way to do it in his particular life. Of course, salvation is also a universal process, as accessible to you as it is to me because we all share the commonalities that unite us as humans. Salvation is, from the point of view of the image of God, a both/and proposition; *both* individualized *and* universally open to all.

This chapter is a brief set of brush strokes at a thickened-up view of salvation. While it focuses on sanctification, it does not mean to deny the significant role for justification. That God the Son entered human life, was born as child, was raised by human parents, grew to maturity in all ways, was crucified, died, and was raised bodily from the dead are all, of course, central to the salvation story, including what we typically call justification by faith. But *here* I want to focus on salvation as a process, a process Jesus-followers commence on while we dwell here in the midst of sin, struggle, disease, and death. Sanctification is as central to salvation as justification is, at least in my estimation. To have faith is to be faithful. But what does

On Becoming Second Incarnations

faithfulness look like? It too will be particularized, but also universal. It will shape us all into the image of God in a fuller, and deeper, and richer way than perhaps we can now conceive of.

In this chapter, then, I turn to the theological underpinnings of spiritual formation or sanctification. Its general goal is to provide an analytical framework for developing a practical approach to becoming Christ-like, an approach that flows out of our uniqueness as human persons made in the image of God.

To begin, we can ask: What is salvation? What is it about? Of course, salvation is not only about getting to heaven or about our sins being forgiven. It is about a whole-life change. Sometimes Protestants tend to divide sanctification from justification. That is less true of Roman Catholics and even less true of the Orthodox. Furthermore, spiritual formation in the Eastern church typically involves the goal of deification. In the West, we prefer the language of sanctification. The two are, arguably, close in meaning, yet those in the Western church—especially, but not only, Protestants—are hesitant to say that humans can become gods. Those in the Eastern church not only use this terminology but celebrate it. The further one is from the deeply iconic and liturgical approach to spiritual formation of the East (through Roman Catholic, Anglican, Reformed, and into the low-church Protestant groups) the less likely it is that one will find talk of deification either helpful or accurate. Unfortunately, those at the extreme opposite end of the spectrum from the East may be losing both a rich way of thinking about spiritual formation, but also some very practical means of attending to our souls. This chapter cannot hope to cover all the ground a full treatment of deification would. Its main task is to consider that if we take the notion that salvation consists in humans becoming gods (like unto God), what theological work must we do to make sense of it?

Some of that work was done in the chapter 2, where I wrote about images and the image of God. While I return to those notions below, I begin by considering two ancient theological statements and use them to frame the discussion. One is from Irenaeus and the other Athanasius, although similar statements were made by Clement of Alexandria, Gregory of Nazianzus, Basil of Caesarea, and Augustine of Hippo. From Irenaeus:

> [T]he Word of God, our Lord Jesus Christ, who did, through His transcendent love, become what we are, that He might bring us to be even what He is Himself.[1]

---

1. Irenaeus, "Book 5, Preface", *Against Heresies*. http://www.ccel.org/ccel/schaff/

Image, Incarnation, and Expansivism

From Athanasius:

> For He was made man that we might be made God.[2]

Of course, neither Irenaeus nor Athanasius (nor any of the others listed) thought we humans could become consubstantial with God. So what then did they mean? How much like God can humans become and in what terms should we think of that deification?

Eastern theologians might be inclined to interpret Irenaeus by Athanasius. Hence, "becoming God" is correlated to "what He is Himself [viz., God]." Westerners, given our hesitancy to say that humans can become God, may read the aphorisms in the opposite direction, Athanasius is interpreted by Irenaeus. So "what He is Himself" (a complete human as we were meant to be) is what is meant by "that we might be made God." To become God, we might say, is to become as much *like* God as humans can become. The early theologians thought it near enough that they used the word "god" to pick out what they had in mind. My question, then, is how alike God can humans become?

The ancients may have talked about becoming God because of Scriptural, image language. On the one hand, humans are made in God's image. On the other hand, the human Jesus is God's image in a sense far richer than we typically think any "regular" human is as a created image of God. Jesus is God, is described as the very image of God, the imprint of God, and, from his own lips, "Whoever has seen me has seen the Father" (John 14:9). How does the image of God that Jesus is relate to the image of God that the rest of us are? I argue that we are second incarnations of God; second because we are just enough like Christ to image God in a rich way, but enough unlike Christ that we only play a second-level role.

Having already reflected on the nature of images in chapter 2, I turn here, in section I, to reflect on a number of biblical passages dealing with the image of God. Section II answers the main question, "how alike God can we humans become?"

---

anf01.ix.vii.i.html.

2. Athanasius, "Section 54," *On the Incarnation.* http://www.ccel.org/ccel/schaff/npnf204.vii.ii.liv.html.

On Becoming Second Incarnations

I

What does Scripture say about images as related to humans and the divine-human Jesus? (I ignore references decrying the making of images or idols.) I found only five explicit mentions of the phrase, "the image of God" (counting Gen 1:26–27 as one). Here are the five (with the references to the image in my italics).

> Genesis 1:26–27. Then God said, "*Let us make humankind in our image, according to our likeness*; and let them have dominion over the fish of the sea, and over the birds of the air, and over the cattle, and over all the wild animals of the earth, and over every creeping thing that creeps upon the earth." *So God created humankind in his image, in the image of God he created them*; male and female he created them.

> Genesis 9:6. Whoever sheds the blood of a human, by a human shall that person's blood be shed; *for in his own image God made humankind.*

> 1 Corinthians 11:7. For a man ought not to have his head veiled, since *he is the image and reflection of God*; but woman is the reflection of man.

> 2 Corinthians 4:4. In their case the god of this world has blinded the minds of the unbelievers, to keep them from seeing the *gospel of the glory of Christ, who is the image of God.*

> Colossians 1:15. *He is the image of the invisible God*, the firstborn of all creation.

I'll refer to these as "image passages."

I found seven related references not using the word "image," but "likeness," "imprint," or otherwise communicating an image of God. I'll refer to them as "likeness passages." Again, I've italicized the likeness or imprint references.

> Genesis 5:1–3. This is the list of the descendants of Adam. When *God created humankind, he made them in the likeness of God*. Male and female he created them, and he blessed them and named them "Humankind" when they were created. When Adam had lived one hundred thirty years, he became *the father of a son in his likeness, according to his image*, and named him Seth.

Image, Incarnation, and Expansivism

John 14:9. Have I been with you all this time, Philip, and you still do not know me? *Whoever has seen me has seen the Father.* How can you say, "Show us the Father"?

Hebrews 1:1–4. Long ago God spoke to our ancestors in many and various ways by the prophets, but in these last days he has spoken to us by a Son, whom he appointed heir of all things, through whom he also created the worlds. *He is the reflection of God's glory and the exact imprint of God's very being,* and he sustains all things by his powerful word. When he had made purification for sins, he sat down at the right hand of the Majesty on high, having become as much superior to angels as the name he has inherited is more excellent than theirs.

Ephesians 4:17–24. Now this I affirm and insist on in the Lord: you must no longer live as the Gentiles live, in the futility of their minds. They are darkened in their understanding, alienated from the life of God because of their ignorance and hardness of heart. They have lost all sensitivity and have abandoned themselves to licentiousness, greedy to practice every kind of impurity. That is not the way you learned Christ! For surely you have heard about him and were taught in him, as truth is in Jesus. You were taught to put away your former way of life, your old self, corrupt and deluded by its lusts, and to be renewed in the spirit of your minds, and to clothe yourselves with the new self, *created according to the likeness of God* in true righteousness and holiness.

Romans 8:3. For God has done what the law, weakened by the flesh, could not do: by *sending his own Son in the likeness of sinful flesh*, and to deal with sin, he condemned sin in the flesh.

Philippians 2:7–8. [B]ut [Christ] emptied himself, taking the form of a slave, *being born in human likeness.* And being found in human form, he humbled himself and became obedient unto death, even death on a cross.

My goal in this section is to reflect on some of the teaching of Scripture on the image of God. Please treat the following comments as a quick dabbling into some thoughts about these passages rather than a full-blown exegesis, the latter of which I don't have the biblical expertise to do. Nevertheless, I believe the observations are generally right and I use them to reflect on the nature of the image of God.

First, I'll set aside 1 Corinthians 11:7. Since it's clear from Genesis that humans, both female and male, are made in God's image, Paul's advice about covering one's head seems not to be fundamentally theological in its aim, but rather aimed at bringing order to an unruly church.

Shifting to Genesis 1, the first thing to note is that humans are *created* or *made* in the image of God, according to God's likeness. We are clearly contingent beings who God planned and then created in the divine image. Yet there is a substantial difference between Western and Eastern theologians on this passage. The Orthodox often claim that "image" and "likeness" are not the same thing. Bishop Kallistos Ware writes:

> According to most of the Greek Fathers, the terms image and likeness do not mean exactly the same thing. "The expression according to the image," wrote John of Damascus, "indicates rationality and freedom, while the expression according to the likeness indicates assimilation to God through virtue." . . . The image, or to use the Greek term the icon, of God signifies man's free will, his reason, his sense of moral responsibility—everything, in short, which marks man out from the animal creation and makes him a person. But the image means more than that. It means that we are God's "offspring" (Acts 27:28), His kin; it means that between us and Him there is a point of contact, an essential similarity. The gulf between creature and Creator is not impassable, for because we are in God's image we can know God and have communion with Him. And if a man makes proper use of this faculty for communion with God, then he will become "like" God, he will acquire the divine likeness; in the words of John Damascene, he will be "assimilated to God through virtue." To acquire the likeness is to be deified, it is to become a "second god," a "god by grace." "I said, you are gods, and all of you sons of the Most High" (Psalm 81:6).[3]

In the West, the distinction between "image" and "likeness" was downplayed by the time of the Reformation. Here are some of the reasons: No "and" joins "in our image" with "after our likeness." Also, in Genesis 1:27 we find simply "in God's image" and no mention of "according to our likeness," and finally, in Genesis 5:1 God made humanity "in the likeness of God." The best explanation (says the "Reformed view") for these data is to say that "in the image" and "after the likeness" refer to the same thing, each clarifying the other.[4] The phrase "in our image, according to our like-

---

3. Ware, "God and Man."
4. Collins, *Genesis 1–4*, 62.

Image, Incarnation, and Expansivism

ness" may be a linguistic Hebraism where a concept is repeated twice with different words to emphasize its importance.[5]

However, several New Testament claims are relevant to this debate. Ephesians 4 indicates that the "new self" Christians are to become is, indeed, "in the likeness of God." No mention is made of the image of God. Could Paul understand the Genesis image/likeness passage along the lines of the Orthodox view noted above? Furthermore, part of the "Reformed argument" appeals to Genesis 5. There humans are described as created in the likeness of God with no mention of the image. Yet Seth, Adam's son, is made in Adam's likeness, according to his image. This reaffirms the parallel to Genesis 1. Is this latter point on the Reformed or the Orthodox side? It may be difficult to see how Adam could have made a distinction in Seth between Adam's image and his likeness, the latter being something to develop spiritually later. Yet perhaps the account is neutral in that regard, for if the image/likeness in us is divided along reason/spiritual growth lines, then that, too, could be passed on from Adam to Seth and, indeed, to all of us. This is consonant with Ware's claim noting that the image of God makes us God's offspring, in a parallel way to Seth's being Adam's offspring.

Let's set the differences aside for now, returning to them below. In either case—Reformed or Orthodox—we know humans are made in God's image at creation and so far forth we should pay attention to the observation that humans are made in the image of *something else,* viz. God. God is clearly the object for the image. Genesis 1 presents an object/image model of the image of God and hence we are dichotomous images of God: copying and hence resembling God, but only resembling one another.

Consider now Genesis 9:6. If taken out of context, it appears to be justifying capital punishment on the basis of the value of humans made in God's image. I don't think the larger context bears that out. Here it is:

> God blessed Noah and his sons, and said to them, "Be fruitful and multiply, and fill the earth. The fear and dread of you shall rest on every animal of the earth, and on every bird of the air, on everything that creeps on the ground, and on all the fish of the sea; into your hand they are delivered. Every moving thing that lives shall be food for you; and just as I gave you the green plants, I give you everything. Only, you shall not eat flesh with its life, that is, its blood. For your own lifeblood I will surely require a reckoning: from every animal I will require it and from human beings, each one for the blood of another, I will require a reckoning for human

---

5. See Ware, "God and Man."

life. Whoever sheds the blood of a human, by a human shall that person's blood be shed; for in his own image God made humankind. And you, be fruitful and multiply, abound on the earth and multiply in it."

Here humans are given "permission" to kill and eat animals, but no animal is to kill a human, not without retribution. This text mirrors the earlier creation story wherein God makes the non-human animals prior to the humans (version one) or makes the animals as possible companions for Adam (version two). In either case, animals are distinct from humans, the latter being made in the image of God. The author appeals to God's image in humans as a way to distinguish them, just as was done earlier in Genesis. Being in the image of God, in this story, is the basis for what distinguishes humans from everything else.

Shifting to the incarnation, we see that it is God's revelation of the divine self to the world, not merely in words, but through a person. Second Corinthians says that unbelief can blind one to "the gospel of the glory of Christ, who is the image of God." Christ is the image of God and that image shows us the glory of Christ. The glory, presumably, is the glory of God (rather than, say, the glory of a human). The use of "glory" here emphasizes that Jesus is God, the "glory of Christ" simply being an equivalent phrase for the "glory of God."

Hebrews 1 reports that God spoke to us through the prophets and later "a Son." God's "speech" through Jesus is not merely words but rather God's *very own being*. Hebrews uses the language of "stamp" or "impress," telling us that the Son is the exact imprint of the very being of God. We are told that the Son is the heir of all things, creator of the worlds, and sustainer of all things by his power. Other translations use the term "exact representation" or "very stamp" instead of "exact imprint." The notion that Christ is the exact image of God comes out in the sense of an object being pressed into clay so that one gets an exact copy of the object. Furthermore, with the image of the "very being" of God, "exactness," and "very" is emphasized. Finally, these things are tied to Christ's role as heir, creator, and sustainer of everything. Christ, the image of God, is indeed God, fully and completely, and, as such, Christ is an image of himself.[6] The author seems to struggle

---

6. Perhaps I press too hard here on the presentational image point. It is, after all, a philosopher's notion and not one the writer of Hebrews would have been familiar with. At the very least, Christ is the image of the Father. Although neither Scripture nor tradition would recognize Christ being an image of himself, the logical point stills stands. But it stands in a complicated way and would need to be extended from a mix of theological

with stating that Jesus is a presentational image of God and not merely a dichotomous image.

Colossians 1:15–20 makes the point more forcefully, for it gives more detail about God's image in Christ.

> He [the Son] is the image of the invisible God, the firstborn of all creation; for in him all things in heaven and on earth were created, things visible and invisible, whether thrones or dominions or rulers or powers—all things have been created through him and for him. He himself is before all things, and in him all things hold together. He is the head of the body, the church; he is the beginning, the firstborn from the dead, so that he might come to have first place in everything. For in him all the fullness of God was pleased to dwell, and through him God was pleased to reconcile to himself all things, whether on earth or in heaven, by making peace through the blood of his cross.

There are at least twelve separate features attributed to Christ in three groups, one listing clearly divine attributions, the second clearly human attributions, and a third listing attributions that could be in one, the other, or both groups. The divine subdivision includes creator of things (including powers) in heaven and earth, all things are through and for him, before all things, all things hold together in him, and from the beginning. The human subdivision contains firstborn of the dead (so he might have first place in everything), reconciler to himself of all things in heaven and earth, and peacemaker through the blood of the cross. The third category includes firstborn of all creation, head of the church, and dwelling place of all the fullness of God. That leaves the image of the invisible God that appears to fit into the human subdivision, but could also fit into divine one. In either and both cases, it frames the entire list.

Assuming the first thing on the list is the most important, Christ's being the image of God is absolutely central to Paul's thinking about Christ's role, both practically (in creation and redemption) and theologically (in the way we should think of Christ). From the fact that Christ is God's image, all the other points unfold. What does it mean in this context to be God's image? Paul's answer includes both divine and human attributes. Some are independent of Christ's incarnation, others dependent on it. Still, the human list includes nothing the rest of us humans have done or been. Jesus, as the image of God, is unique.

---

and philosophical thinking.

John overall takes a different tack, one not fitting so well the image language. In John 14:9 Jesus says: "Have I been with you all this time, Philip, and you still do not know me? Whoever has seen me has seen the Father. How can you say, 'Show us the Father?'" Jesus—the walking, talking, laughing, sad, vulnerable, and ultimately the crucified and resurrected Jesus—doesn't merely reveal the Father. There is a virtual *identity* claim (and elsewhere in John Jesus says "I and the Father are one"). See me, see the Father. There's no mention of Jesus as the image of God. But if we take the Johannine "seeing" passages as "image passages," it seems very clear that the image Jesus is is not merely dichotomous. If Jesus is a dichotomous image of the Father (as a picture of my father is an image of him) then Jesus is not really the Father and one is not seeing the Father when one sees the Son. So far forth that is true since God the Son is not God the Father, following a trinitarian interpretation. But Jesus seems to be saying simply that when one sees him one sees God. That requires, if we take Jesus to be the image of God, a presentational understanding of image. Otherwise we get an unorthodox view of Jesus.

The Chalcedon confession, the orthodox view, says:

> Following the holy fathers, we all with one consent teach men to confess one and the same Son, our Lord Jesus Christ, the same perfect in Godhead and also perfect in Manhood; truly God and truly man, of a reasonable [rational] soul and body; consubstantial [coequal] with the Father according to the Godhead, and consubstantial with us according to the Manhood; in all things like unto us, without sin, begotten before all ages of the Father according to the Godhead, and in these latter days, for us and for our salvation, born of the Virgin Mary, the Mother of God, according to the Manhood; one and the same Christ, Son, Lord, Only-begotten, to be acknowledged in two natures, *Inconfusedly, unchangeably, indivisibly, inseparably;* the distinction of natures being by no means taken away by the union but rather the property of each nature being preserved, and concurring in one Person and one Subsistence, not parted or divided into two Persons, but one and the same Son, and only-begotten, God the Word, the Lord Jesus Christ; as the prophets from the beginning [have declared] concerning him, and the Lord Jesus Christ himself has taught us, and the Creed of the holy Fathers has handed down to us.[7]

---

7. See Schaff, "Section 2. The Chalcedonian Statement."

Image, Incarnation, and Expansivism

The two natures of Christ (divine and human) are affirmed in the singular personhood of Christ. Focusing on Christ's humanity, we find it consubstantial with humans. "Consubstantial" is the same term describing the divine nature of Christ's relationship with God the Father. Christ is like us in all things except sin (sin being adventitious to human beings). Since being made in the image of God is what makes us human, then Jesus has to be made in God's image as well. So Jesus is both *made* in the image of God (dichotomous) and *is* the image of God (presentational).

Romans 8 says God has done what the law, weakened by the flesh, could not do. By sending his own Son in the likeness of sinful flesh to deal with sin, God condemned sin in the flesh. God's law is weakened by the flesh and not strong enough to overcome sin. Presumably this is because it is left up to "regular" humans to fulfill the law, which we can't or don't do. The Son, however, is not weakened by flesh even though sent in the likeness of that very same sinful flesh. Paul uses "likeness" rather than "image" language here. Jesus is "merely" in the likeness of sinful flesh; that is, he does not necessarily share all the properties of sinful flesh. One important way he does not is, of course, that he is without sin. Being in the likeness of sinful flesh allows Jesus to be a general typifying image of the set of all humans. But Jesus is also the ideal typifying human, for he better epitomizes humans *as they are supposed to be* than any other human would be able to do.

Paul indicates that the divine presence in human flesh condemns the sin and overcomes it. In terms of the incarnation, Jesus is in the likeness of sinful flesh, but does not sin. There is some support here for the Orthodox view that the likeness of God in us is that part open to virtuous development. Because we sinned, we moved ourselves away from the (true) likeness of God. When Jesus comes in the likeness of sinful flesh, he comes *having to learn how to be a virtuous human* just as Adam would have. This is consonant with Luke 2:52, which tells us that Jesus increased in wisdom and in years, and in divine and human favor. Jesus had to learn, just like the rest of us, how to be in the likeness of God (rather than sin) by being fully (or becoming fully) in the likeness of the flesh *as God intended it*. At the fall we chose to become less than fully human—less aligned with God—and sinful in our flesh.

This may sound as if Jesus' being divine was not important; as if a merely human Jesus could will himself to follow God. That is not so. God is essential to the salvific process. Because God becomes the *unified divine-human person*, Jesus is able to be the likeness of God (in the Orthodox sense) as a human. The presence of God is the power Jesus needs as a human to choose toward God. Indeed, if the Orthodox are right, for humans to come into the appropriate relationship with God, God must show us how to do it. Jesus shows us by being the likeness, something no humans had done on their own. Being made in God's image is not enough. While granting us grounds as the offspring of God, we have to use those grounds to choose toward God, something we can do only by grace since we can't do it by nature.

Here we risk tipping the scale the other direction; as if the divine might be more central than the human. That is a mistake, a tendency balanced by Philippians 2:5–11.

> Let the same mind be in you that was in Christ Jesus, who, though he was in the form of God, did not regard equality with God as something to be exploited, but emptied himself, taking the form of a slave, being born in human likeness. And being found in human form, he humbled himself and became obedient to the point of death—even death on a cross. Therefore God also highly exalted him and gave him the name that is above every name, so that at the name of Jesus every knee should bend, in heaven and on earth and under the earth, and every tongue should confess that Jesus Christ is Lord, to the glory of God the Father.

Christ empties himself of the divine and enters into the likeness of humans, even to the point of death. We too need to become humble enough to die, both to our own desires and, in fact, literally.[8]

II

How alike can a human become to God? To answer that question, we'll have to look at how alike God became to a human. We typically know God through material objects, whether it is the wonders of nature reflecting God's glory, the love of God through the love our parents, the written text

---

8. The only remaining reference to the likeness of God is in James 3 where the phrase "those made in the likeness of God" is apparently a reference to humans. We praise God but curse humans with the very same tongue. Who can tame it? There appears to be little new in this reference that is not found in the others discussed. In fact, James's use of the phrase appears to be simply a flourish, a way to talk about humans, whereas his main point is about taming the tongue.

of Scripture, or through Jesus the incarnate God. So it is appropriate to focus on the notion of the image of God, for it is images that we experience.[9]

We humans are made in the dichotomous image of God; we are copies of God with God being both the causal source of the copy as well as being present to the causal chain by which the copy is made. Jesus too, as a human, is the dichotomous image of God. But Jesus is also the presentational image of God's very being. Is the image of God in Jesus the same as the image of God in the rest of the human race? If it is, Jesus must be *created* or *made* in the image of God just as the rest of us. Unfortunately, the two references to Christ as the (presentational) image of God fail to mention that he is *made* in the image. In fact, if Jesus were *merely* made in the image of God, he would merely be a dichotomous image and not a presentational image. Jesus wouldn't be God any more than the rest of us humans are. So how can a human also be God?

Jesus certainly is made in the image of God as we are (that's what being a human is), but there are a number of important differences about Jesus in that regard. While we are made in God's (dichotomous) image, we are made from nothing (or from finite stuff—dirt, in the Genesis story—which in turn is made from nothing). God is the object and humans the copy. The human Jesus is not made from nothing, but rather the pre-existing God *is made into a human* while retaining the divine nature. While that is peculiar enough, it's not my focus at present. Rather, it is the more specific issue that a divine entity is made into the (dichotomous) image *of that very same object*. While it is not so hard to see how Christ can be his own presentational image, it is difficult to see how an object can be its own dichotomous image.

It is tempting to say that perhaps Jesus can be both the presentational image (being divine) and the dichotomous image (being human). That would keep the two natures of Christ separate enough not to contradict Chalcedon. But it creates another issue. The human Jesus is the presentational image of God—if you've seen me, you've seen the Father. So radical a separation of the human and the divine in Christ undermines Chalcedon's claim that Jesus is one person. Jesus is a divine-human person with two natures united into one person. When we see Jesus, we do not see two aspects of Jesus but one, united person. The neat division of Christ into the human dichotomous image and the divine presentational image undermines the doctrine of the incarnation.

---

9. There are, of course, exceptions to this. Nonetheless, images are a fundamental way in which we come to understand God.

But another peculiarity about Jesus arises. Since humans pre-exist the human Jesus, and Jesus is made human (from, so to speak, divine stuff), it seems that God takes humans as a model for what Jesus is to be like. Hence Jesus is, unlike the rest of us, made in the (dichotomous) image *of humans*. Some care is needed here, for in the sense that certain universal properties are instantiated in humans (reason, emotion, will, creativity, etc.) we are all made in the "image" of humans. One requirement for dichotomous images is informational sharing between object and image, including natural dichotomous imaging via genetic coding. In this regard, we are all (save Adam) copies of other humans. In short, we are the natural kind "human," our genetic coding making it so. So it is with Jesus. But that, arguably, is not what Scripture means when it says humans are made in the image of God. Genetic coding is the mechanism, perhaps, by which human nature is passed on from generation to generation, but God does not make Adam simply by instantiating some abstract properties (those essential to human persons). God makes Adam unique, Eve unique, and everyone that follows unique. Even though God may use genetic coding to pass on thin essential properties that we all share and in virtue of which we are in the kind "human," those are thickened up in quite unique ways because of our historical, cultural, and conceptual-schematic situations. I argued earlier that being unique is just as much a part of the essence of human persons as being volitional, creative, emotional, or rational. That is, I believe, the real importance of the (dichotomous) image-language of Scripture. Each of us is made by God, we copy God, and hence resemble God. Though we resemble each other because of the thin essential properties we share, we are also unique and do not always resemble one another at "thicker" levels, but we always resemble God and that is the glory of the image of God in us.

So we are all copies of God, sharing the essence of humanity, but individually unique in bearing a different resemblance to God than any of our sisters and brothers. How then is Jesus made in the image of humans? Although Jesus certainly does have the thin essence of humanity, the imprint of humanness from Mary, something more is involved. For that, we need to look at Jesus' uniqueness as against the rest of us and not merely his commonalities with the rest of us.

Returning to some observations from chapter 2, just as I was born of my parents, lived in my hometown, had the friends I did, etc.—in short, just as I had a history that made me the unique instantiation of the human essence that I am, so did Jesus. He was born of Mary, raised by Mary and

Image, Incarnation, and Expansivism

Joseph, spent time in the temple at twelve years of age, and was baptized by John. Jesus' history, however, includes the fact that he pre-existed his earthly life.[10] When the Son was made human, his divine being was made flesh, one person with two natures. Part of his history, a history that continues as history when the Son is made human, is that he is God. Hence, when we see the human Jesus we are seeing God, just as when you see me, you are seeing my history. Of course, you are not seeing it in detail. You are seeing the result, the peculiar, particular instantiation of the human essence that has come to be me. Just as you don't see the fact that I was born of the parents I was born of, so we don't see the fact that Jesus is God. But such facts are open to discovery in social relationship. As you get to know me, you get to know that my parents were Jean and Norm. So with Jesus. As people get to know him, they come to realize that *this human is also God*. The presentational image that Jesus is of God is now combined with the presentational image of his humanity, the unique human Jesus is. So being the dichotomous image of God as a human merges in Jesus with his presentational image as God to become the unique divine-human Jesus is.

His uniqueness includes his being made in the image of humanity, which in turn is the image of God. What sense of "image" do I mean when I say Jesus is made in the image of humanity? The typifying image. Typifying images come in two forms, general and ideal. Jesus is the general image of humanity in the same way any of us is, sharing thin essential properties. Whatever properties make us human, we all have them. What are those properties? The potential list is long, including rationality, emotional richness, creativity, and volition. I won't settle on a final list. Instead I turn to one possibility that we might think typifies humanity but does not. Sin. All humans have sinned, except one.[11] Being sinful is *not* part of the human essence.

Adam and Eve were not sinful before the fall, yet they were human. But they were not ideal humans. In Western theology, humans were made morally perfect and we fell from that perfection into sin. The image of God and the likeness of God are largely treated as the same thing. In Eastern theology, the image and the likeness are separated. The image of God includes our rationality, volition, and so forth, whereas our likeness to God

---

10. By using the term "history" here and in the next few sentences, I do not mean to take a stand one way or another on whether God is atemporal.

11. Two, if you count Mary, but she, being only human, is like the rest of us, made holy by grace and not by nature.

is our capacity for virtue, for being, in short, like God in that way. We were created more like children who needed to mature into the likeness of God than fully formed adults. We were innocent as children are innocent rather than innocent as a morally perfect adult would be innocent. We had to live our lives in our difficult circumstances and God wanted us to choose the divine way, will, and goodness rather than our own version of those things. We failed to do so. Jesus, however, does choose the right way. He becomes the one human who consistently chooses to deny his own human will, his self-centered will, and to rely on God for both the knowledge of, and the power to do, God's will. It is not just that Jesus does the things God wants (the particular actions), but he does them with the attitude of God. His human will thus is united with the divine will. He is thus *by nature* the human God had planned for Adam and Eve to be. As he copies humanity, he ideally typifies what humanity can be.

So Jesus is both the general and the ideal typifying image of humans. He shares with us all the things common and essential to humans. Sin is not on that list of properties. You and I would be good general typifying images of humanity because we have the same "thin" essential properties. But only Jesus is the *ideal* typifying image of humanity, for only he is by nature without sin. Jesus comes with the divine power to choose the right thing, to move toward the likeness of God. Indeed, as he matures as a human person, he is able to do just that, to be fully in the likeness of God *as a human*. In choosing to be incarnated, God chooses the sort of human he wants to be. He picks a model, an object, and becomes a presentational image of that object. It is as if God looked through a window at humans and saw both their potential and their weakness. In forming the divine self into human being, he picks only the essential properties and hence becomes a general typifying image of all humans. But in rejecting our sinfulness—remember that to resemble includes the possibility of difference—he also becomes the ideal typifying image. But the window through which God views humanity becomes a mirror which, instead of Jesus being the object and the mirror reflection the image, what's in the mirror (us) becomes the object and Jesus the image, *but the improved, mature image*. Here the image becomes better than the object. To be less metaphorical, the object picked is, one supposes, the mental image God had all along of what the mature, fully human person was to be, not merely in the image, but also the likeness of God. Jesus then becomes the ideal typifying image of humanity.

Image, Incarnation, and Expansivism

Each of us is to model ourselves on Jesus. Jesus is to be our "likeness model." What was Jesus like, how did he get to be the divine ideal typifying image in human flesh? By his choosing *as a human* not to follow his own desires or will (self-protective, self-indulgent, etc.) but to follow God's desires or will. As indicated above, will can be understood both as content and as attitude; as a list of things God wants us to do or as an attitude with which we act. Jesus takes on both. Properly understood, God's will is not onerous. One can do the will of another without joy, by submitting oneself to the will of another. A slave, for example, can do the will of his master but not do it out of his own sense of will. Presumably Jesus learns not to do God's will as something onerous but with the same spirit in which it is intended, the spirit of love. We are to mold our wills to God's, not merely as a duty to be done, but as a loving response. We can say that the human will is amalgamated with the will of God, looking the same direction, with the same attitude and same desire, as God. As one learns submission, one learns to love. That is what Jesus does as a human. He learns to submit, not with a negative sense of doing his duty, but in the positive sense of forming his human will to be the will of love. By maturing in the context of the challenging world into which Jesus is placed, he learns to be like God.[12] We are to do the very same thing as Jesus. We learn humility by denying our own desires and taking up the same vision as God has, the vision of love. Adam was not able to do that in his own strength. He needed God's help and example. Jesus provides that divine help and example. What Jesus had by nature, we can have by grace, God's love exemplified in Jesus Christ by the power of the Holy Spirit.

How does all this fit together? Jesus is the presentational image of God, not merely because he is God, but because he is God enrobed in flesh, the particular human person he is, born of Mary, raised in Palestine, etc. God incarnate is both a copy of God (dichotomous—made as we are in all ways without sin) and a copy of humans (ideal typifying—the best of what humans ought to be). In his unified person—when the dual wills and natures of Christ are united in one person—we see God. The actual presentational image of God is in front of us, the single-membered set of divine-human being imaging himself. But as a human, he is also the member of a larger set, the set of humans. We share the image of God in that we all copy God

---

12. Were there more space, we could reflect on the fact that obligations and duties—the stuff of human morality—will presumably fade away in the kingdom, replaced by gift-giving and sharing with our sisters and brothers.

dichotomously and uniquely and we image God in terms of our shared essence as well.

How does a human become God? God becomes human so humans can become God. Part of Jesus' being the presentational image of God and thus God himself is that Jesus is the unique divine-human person. To see Jesus is to see God. Can the same be true of us; is it possible for a human to be such that to see the human is to see God? Yes. Not, of course, in the consubstantial sense that Jesus is. But yes in terms of our individual unique selves learning to live out the full will of God, just as Jesus did. Just as Jesus is the ideal typifying image of humans, so can we become. We can be just like Jesus in that our human will can be amalgamated with the divine will. Such a person is a saint; to see a saint act and live is to see God. Just as when you see me, you see my presentational self, with all my history, so when you see Jesus, you see his divinity. But because Jesus becomes the ideal typifying image of humanity, he becomes what we are to become, the likeness of God as a human. What he is by nature, we become by grace.

We become, in short, what we might describe as second incarnations of God. God becomes so present in us via his will being amalgamated with our wills that to see us is to see the divine. But having God's will so closely aligned or even identified with ours does not make us consubstantial with God. It makes us incarnations of God of a second-order. Jesus is God first and incarnated God second. We are humans first, and incarnations of God second. He is God and the ideal typifying human by nature, we are (fallen) humans first and we become ideal typifying humans by grace. When we arrive there, we are incarnations of God's will.

Are we presentational images of God? Not in the full sense Jesus is, but because God's image in us is as much about our uniqueness as it is about our commonalities, as we journey toward God and toward being God's likenesses, we journey toward being presentational images of God's will in our unique ways. That is as close to being God as humans are capable of being: second incarnations in history of the divine will. The divine will is love and we can become totally loving beings, and we do so in history.

Again from Irenaeus: "[T]he Word of God, our Lord Jesus Christ, who did, through His transcendent love, become what we are, that He might bring us to be even what He is Himself."[13] And from Athanasius: "For He was made man that we might be made God."[14] If we read the clause from

---

13. Irenaeus, *Against Heresies*, Book 5, Preface.
14. Athanasius, *On the Incarnation*, section 54.

Image, Incarnation, and Expansivism

Irenaeus "bring us to be even what He is Himself" through the eyes of Athanasius's clause "that we might be made God" then it appears on the surface that humans will, in the salvific economy, become God. I've argued that, as incarnations of God's will (when we are formed into the sorts of beings God intended us to be) we become like God; as close to God as humans can be. We do that only as incarnations of God's will, however, and not as the pre-existing God. Jesus is God always. In his humanity he is both God and takes on the likeness of God by taking on the likeness of ideal humans. We can take on the likeness of God and as such become second incarnations. We become presentational images of God, like Jesus, but not identical in all ways. It is only in our human ways that this is accomplished by grace. Jesus has it by nature.

Salvation, then, turns out to be a particularized process, localized to the particular human I am, with the particular history I have. So it is with you and your particular history and so it is everyone and their particular histories. But we move into salvation because Jesus shows us the way to do it in his particular life. Of course, salvation is also a universal process, as accessible to you as it is to me because we all share the commonalities that unite us together as humans. Salvation is, from the point of view of the image of God, a both/and proposition; both individualized and universally open to all. That is, indeed, expansively good news.

———————— Appendix ————————

Theistic Irrealism's Ancestors

Theistic irrealism is a complex theory of ontological pluralism. As is appropriate to its project, it builds on the other theories, mainly those of Steven Hales, Michael Lynch, and Nelson Goodman. Theistic irrealism was first presented in book form in my *Make/Believing the World(s)*. Here I present, in very truncated form, a summary of the building blocks of that book. One can read the present book, I hope, without reference to the technical details presented here. But for those who are interested, the following will provide some further background. There are three sections, devoted consecutively to Hales, Lynch, and Goodman.

I

Steven Hales provides an account of (what he calls) "relativist" logic that first limits the claims of relativism and second shows why global relativism is self-refuting while a more limited relativism need not be. While I prefer the term "pluralist," I've left this summary in the terms he prefers. In the end, the logical framework he develops for relativism will support the type of pluralistic ontology I propose.

To begin, Hales compares "everything is relative" to "everything is possible." This comparison is important, for although it is false that everything is possible, it is clearly true that everything true is possibly true. In

Appendix

contrast, while it is false that everything is relative, it is true that everything true is relatively true. Hales writes:

> Suppose that everything is possible. That is, for all Φ, $\Diamond\Phi$. Allow Φ to be "it is necessarily not true that everything is possible." Then the following turns out to be true: possibly, it is necessarily not true that everything is possible. A well-known theorem in modal system S5 tells us that whatever is possibly necessary is necessary. We can thereby conclude that it is necessarily not true that everything is possible. Thus, by reductio, it cannot be the case that everything is possible. So what should we do? Should we abandon all talk of modality, give up possibility and necessity, and purge ourselves of possible worlds? Of course not. . . . No one is seriously prepared to claim that everything is possible. Yet everyone *is* prepared to affirm this thesis: everything true is possibly true [italics his].[1]

This last thesis, Hales notes, does not entail that nothing is necessarily true. Possible truth is not mere possibility. Something's being possibly true doesn't rule out its being necessarily true. Furthermore, possible truth is not a "cheap" version of real or actual truth.

Hales then introduces two other operators ♦ and ■. The former indexes sentences to perspectives so that ♦Φ is to be read: "it is relatively true (true in some perspective) that Φ." The latter operator is an "absolute" operator so that ■Φ is to be read: "it is absolutely true (true in all perspectives) that Φ." If we then accept the S5-like theorem that whatever is relatively absolute is absolute (for all Φ, ♦■$\Phi \Rightarrow$ ■Φ) (he calls this ***P*** and we take "it is absolutely not true that everything is relative" as a substitution instance of Φ, we get that it is absolutely not true that everything is relative. This, of course, shows global relativism self-refuting.

Hales's argument rests heavily on the truth of ***P*** and he presents a good case for its truth. The gist is this. One of the things global relativists say is that relativism is merely relatively true, that is, true in some perspectives and not true in others. But how would this work? Hales takes the latter case first, viz., the position that relativism is not true in some perspectives. In that perspective absolutism (not relativism) is true. Absolutism claims that some proposition has the same truth-value in all perspectives. Hales calls this situation *p*. In *p*, there is some Φ such that ■Φ. But how could *p* contain such a proposition? Φ could not be the thesis of absolutism itself. The reason is that *ex hypothesi* there are perspectives in which absolutism is

---

1. Hales, *Relativism*, 99–100.

not true and relativism is. On the other hand, Φ could not be the thesis of relativism. Again, this is the case since *ex hypothesi* there are perspectives in which relativism is not true. Other candidates for Φ are in no better shape, since—given the assumption that there are perspectives in which relativism is true—it must be the case that the truth-value of every proposition Φ will vary across perspectives. Thus, no proposition is true in all perspectives. For each proposition it is true in some perspectives and not in others. But it follows then that relativism is true in all perspectives. This, as Hales shows, entails that relativism in not true. Relativism can be neither absolutely nor relatively true and so the claim "everything is relative" must be false.[2] Of the argument just described, Hales writes that

> we considered the option of relativism being relatively not true. Therefore, in some perspective there was a proposition Φ that was absolutely true. Formally: ◆■Φ. Yet it turned out that there could not be such a proposition since the assumption of relativism prevented any proposition from being true in all perspectives. In other words, there could not be a Φ such that ■ Φ. This is why ◆■ Φ could not be true. The form underlying this argument is modus tollens. The conditional relied on is none other than the S5-like principle *P*: ◆■ Φ⇒■ Φ. The preceding argument does not constitute a formal proof that *P* is true; rather it is a set of semantical considerations designed to uncover the intuition that *P*. It is a tacit acceptance of *P* that I suspect under girds many rejections of "relativism is absolutely false" as being merely true relatively.[3]

Thus, global relativism is false and the principle that undergirds the self-refutation objection to global relativism is *P*.

What then is the relativist to say? Is she or he to give up on relativism? Hales says, no, at least not for that reason. Just as one shouldn't give up on possible world semantics because one rejects "everything is possible," we shouldn't give up on relativism because it turns out that "everything is relative" is false. Just as "everything is possible" runs afoul the theorem that ◊□ Φ⇒□ Φ, "everything is relative" runs afoul *P*. But "everything true is possibly true" does not run afoul ◊□ Φ⇒□ Φ, and neither does "everything true is relatively true does not run afoul *P*. Hales writes:

> There is nothing self-contradictory or paradoxical about the claim that everything true is relatively true, just as there is no puzzle

---

2. Ibid., 101.
3. Ibid., 101, 102

engendered by the claim that whatever is true is possibly true. As in the case of alethic modality, it is entirely consistent for the new-and-improved relativist to hold that some propositions are absolutely true, and that perspectival truth is every bit as decent and upstanding as "real" truth. Indeed, "real" truth is just truth in this perspective, just as actual truth is truth in this world. Absolute truth turns out to be truth in all perspectives, just as necessary truth is truth in all worlds. For the relativist it will be nonsense to talk about truth outside of the structure of perspectives—that is, nonperspectival or extraperspectival truth. However, this stricture should be no scarier than forbidding talk of truth outside the structure of worlds, once we have accepted possible world semantics.[4]

Relativism, of this limited sort, does not fall prey to the challenge of self-refutation.

Hales notes several further issues. Some relativists might be loath to accept *P* for it shows that their view is false. But *P*'s rejection leaves the relativist to answer the self-refutation problem. It seems not a good approach for the relativist just to ignore it. Second, some relativists might be bothered by the fact that the view Hales develops is consistent with all truths being absolutely so and that theorems such as *P* are absolutely true. But, says Hales, relativists should be pleased that the view developed is consistent with many propositions being merely relatively true and not absolutely so. Hales furthermore notes a further advantage of his position viz., relativism's truth doesn't just fall out of the logic. Relativism needs to argue for its claims.

II

Following Michael Lynch, let's say a worldview is an organic whole. The whole's parts can be understood in relation to their functions inside the whole. The parts include our beliefs, our concepts used to form our beliefs, the interests we have in forming the concepts, the values that guide those interests, and the underlying practices and capacities that limit and define our cognitive production and intake. One part of any given worldview is the conceptual scheme it employs.[5] There are, we might say, many worldviews

---

4. Ibid., 102, 103.
5. Ibid., 51.

and it is out of those worldviews—in particular the conceptual schematic aspects of worldviews—that we generate the many ways the World is or what I'll call "worlds." I'll use the term "World" to designate the underlying, Kantian-like "noumenal" that we inherit from God. The term "worlds" I'll reserve for the plural ways in which we construct that World.

I say that we "generate" or "make" worlds. Of course, many of our concepts do not come and go at will, so since "generating" or "making" worlds seems to imply an active rather than a passive role on our part, it seems that we don't actually generate or make the ways the World is. Here I disagree with the description of pluralism Lynch suggests and side more with Nelson Goodman, who compares making things with concepts to making things with our hands. The former is much more difficult than the latter. "Making right world-versions—or making worlds—is harder than making chairs or planes, and failure is common largely because all we have available is scrap material recycled from old and stubborn worlds. Our having done no better or worse is no evidence that chairs or planes or worlds are found rather than made."[6]

However, Lynch is partly right when he says the "ebb and flow of our concepts more often takes place well beneath the surface of our thought." The ebb and flow does often take place beneath the surface of our thought, but I think it also often takes place at the surface as well, as when we explicitly theorize, or make art, or invent new things.

One significant aspect of a worldview is its conceptual scheme. Again following Lynch, I use what he calls a "Wittgensteinian model" of a conceptual scheme. He says, following Peter Strawson, that basic concepts are

a. Concepts the grasping of which are presupposed in employing a large number of our other, more specific concepts.

b. Such concepts are *highly general*—many other concepts naturally fall under them without them falling naturally under any other concept.

c. They are *irreducible* for they can't be defined away, without circularity, in terms of those other concepts.

Lynch adds to the Strawson account that

d. Basic concepts are *significant* in that they play important roles within our conceptual scheme. A concept will not be basic unless it matters

6. Goodman, *Of Mind*, 145.

Appendix

to me, unless going without the concept would severely limit and reshape our conceptual life to the point of unrecognizability[7]

Basic concepts make up the "riverbed" propositions of Wittgenstein's notion of a conceptual scheme, playing a normative role within one's worldview. According to the Wittgensteinian model, conceptual schemes have four core aspects:

a. Conceptual schemes are networks of general and specific concepts used in the propositions we express in language and in thought. Concepts thus are understood functionally, open to various ontological interpretations as to what plays the role of concept.
b. Conceptual schemes differ when they don't share the same basic concepts.
c. Conceptual schemes are consistent with fuzzy analytical/synthetic and related distinctions.
d. Conceptual schemes are only structurally foundationalist; that is, basic concepts are contextually as opposed to absolutely basic.

Having before us an account of conceptual schemes, we need to understand concepts. Lynch proposes a pair of related notions, the crystalline/fluid picture of concepts and the minimal/robust notions of concepts. Let's begin with the basic notion of a concept. He writes that "concepts are the constituents of propositions, whatever they turn out to be. Concepts compose our thoughts; in short, a concept is a particular way of thinking about something or other. So to *have a concept* involves understanding or 'seeing' something a certain way, and moreover it implies the possession of certain abilities [italics his]."[8]

The crystalline picture of concepts suggests that concepts are quite clear and clearly applicable. When a concept is absolutely determinate, its boundaries are always and everywhere precise. This picture of concepts is behind the notion that there are necessary and sufficient conditions for the application of a concept. In contrast, the fluid picture of concepts suggests that concepts are not absolutely determinate but elastic and flexible. Fluid concepts are open to future application, and need not be absolutely determinate. We are not confused about their application, but concepts are not

---

7. Lynch, *Truth*, 44.
8. Ibid., 56.

absolutely determinate or closed. They do not have a fixed use in every possible situation. On the fluid picture of concepts, it makes little sense to talk of "the" concept of one thing or another. Inconsistent applications of a concept occur regularly in everyday discourse.

Lynch continues his discussion by distinguishing between minimal and robust concepts. A minimal concept of F "floats free" of (most) metaphysical questions surrounding Fs. As such, a minimal concept is a way of thinking about something neutrally regarding its ontological nature. A robust concept of F is a concept whose ordinary use consists of a commitment to some particular ontological view of Fs.[9] We can use the term "mind" minimally whether we are materialists or dualists, for example. In a conversation between two philosophers, it can be seen that while they disagree about what the mind is, they both agree that they are speaking of the same thing. Epistemic justification is another example. The generally characterized notion of epistemic justification (its minimal concept) deals with what it is plus truth that gives us knowledge, while operative notions of epistemic justification can be spelled out in internalist or externalist ways, giving a more robust concept. So, robust concepts are enrichments or extensions of the more minimal concepts.

One important issue for pluralism is how these two distinctions—crystalline vs. fluid, minimal vs. robust—are applied to objects, existence, and truth. These three concepts are themselves fluid, says Lynch. It is their fluidity that can solve a number of issues for the pluralist who wants to hold alethic realism.

The absolutist will say that the concept of an object must be absolute and determinate since the concept of existence is absolute and determinate. Thus, metaphysical questions about what there is can be given absolute answers. So the absolutist, being driven by a crystalline picture of concepts, claims that our notions of objecthood and existence are fixed and determinate. Lynch rejects that view. The problem with distinguishing existing from nonexisting objects is that there is no property that all existing objects share, for there are no objects that do not exist. Since there can be no nonexisting objects, there could be no property that would distinguish existing from nonexisting objects or exclude some objects from the class of existing objects.[10] But then if existence is not an absolute concept, then neither is the concept of object absolute. Both existence and object are concepts flex-

---

9. Ibid., 56.
10. Ibid., 84.

Appendix

ible, fluid, and open. We learn them by reference to certain paradigms, but then we extend them beyond the paradigms. In other words, Lynch makes the Kantian point that existence is not a property. So not only is there no essence to existence but existence itself is not a property. The upshot of Lynch's discussion is that what exists, that is, what objects there are, can be dependent upon the conceptual scheme one has without undermining a fairly stable, although fluid, concept of existence and objecthood. These concepts are open and fluid, but not arbitrary or equivocal.

What about truth? One significant difference between the concept of truth and the concept of existence is that truth, according to Lynch, is a property and in particular a property that some propositions have and some do not. While there are no nonexistent objects, there are nontrue propositions. Truth being a property is, indeed, required for a realist account of truth according to Lynch. He says that the T-Schema—i.e., the proposition that *p is true if and only if p*—is a necessary truth.[11] Combining the T-schema with the principle that *things are as the proposition that p says they are if and only if p*, we get "MR (minimal realism)."[12]

> MR: The proposition that p is true if, and only if, things are as the proposition that p says they are.

This view is not deflationary theory. He claims that instances of the T-schema and minimal realism are conceptual truths, but that this does not entail that truth is not a property or that "p" and "the proposition that p is true" are synonymous. Truth, in short, is a real property. Furthermore, MR is a minimal theory in that it lacks the grander metaphysical implications of the correspondence theory, which is a more robust version of the minimal account of truth. In particular, while the correspondence theory suggests an absolutely strict structural relationship between propositions and scheme-independent facts, the minimalist theory does nothing of the sort. Hence, MR is compatible with being taken in the direction of a correspondence theory, but does not entail it. Nor does the minimalist theory conflict with metaphysical pluralism, for it is open to there being truths under different conceptual schemes.

Finally, it is important to note that this metaphysically "thin" account of truth requires an equally metaphysically thin account of proposition and fact. If any instance of the T-schema is necessarily true then there are

11. Ibid., 112.
12. Ibid., 126.

Theistic Irrealism's Ancestors

propositions if there are any truths at all. Nevertheless, granting the existence of propositions doesn't force one to take a stand on their metaphysical nature.[13]

Likewise with facts. The minimal alethic realist will admit that the F-Schema—i.e., *it is a fact that p if and only if p*—together with the T-schema gives us:

> It is a fact that p if, and only if, it is true that p.

But again, the minimalist about truth can remain neutral with regard to the ontological nature of facts. A fact turns out to be whatever is the case, and of course, what is the case is so within the confines of a conceptual scheme.

Relying on Alston, who in turn relies on Putnam and Kripke, a distinction can be made between truth as a concept and truth as a property. Thus, one can grasp the minimalist concept of truth and see that it is consistent with a richer, more substantive account of the property. Hence, "armed with the distinction between concept and property, it would seem that we can make sense of alethic pluralism. Simply put, the minimal realist can hold that there is only one concept of truth but allow that there may be more than one property that fits the constraints marked out by the concept. In this way, the nature of truth can vary across conceptual schemes even as a single, univocal concept of truth is being shared in those same schemes."[14] The minimal realist account of truth is both fluid and stable: fluid because it can be enriched in a variety of contexts and stable because even the more robust accounts are extensions of the basic, minimal account.

In summary, Lynch holds that truth is a property some propositions have while others don't. The minimal concept of truth gives us this much. What it does not give us is the nature of truth, or what the property's "fleshed out" account will be in any given conceptual scheme. While we know, simply from reflecting on the concept of truth, that something's being true is enough to tell us that the thing has the property of truth, what we do not know is what the property will look like in a given conceptual scheme, that is, when robustly filled out. So according to Lynch's ontological pluralism, humans contribute to the World via the various worldviews we hold. One part of a worldview is a conceptual scheme. A conceptual scheme includes concepts that are the constituents of propositions. Concepts are either thick or thin. Thin concepts, which may be shared across conceptual schemes,

13. Ibid., 127.
14. Ibid., 130.

Appendix

are "thickened up" within a worldview *cum* conceptual scheme and because of that thickening, the objects correlated to that conceptual scheme are distinct from the objects correlated to other (competing) conceptual schemes. Across these conceptual schemes, however, a realist alethic theory holds.

There are two faces to pluralism, says Lynch. The first is content relativism. In speaking of assertions, we can ask about their content. The pluralist will say that the content of an assertion is relative to a worldview *cum* conceptual scheme. In contrast, content absolutism says that "what we say or think on some occasion—the proposition we express—is not relative to any worldview, perspective, or conceptual scheme."[15] The second face of pluralism is fact relativism. This is most easily introduced in contrast to fact absolutism, which says two things: first, the totality of facts, should it exist, is necessarily unique and nonrelative; second, facts are external to worldview. Necessarily there can be one and only one totality of facts; one and only one way the world is.[16] In contrast, fact relativism claims that facts are "internal to conceptual schemes, or ways of dividing the world into objects, among which there can be equally acceptable alternatives."[17] What there is in the World is there only within the context of a conceptual scheme. There is no scheme-neutral way of making a report about the world.[18]

However, it doesn't follow that conceptual schemes don't overlap; conceptual schemes need not be incommensurable. Schemes are incommensurable "only to the degree to which they do not share concepts, basic concepts in particular."[19] Thus, people speaking from one scheme to another can understand one another.[20] Further, that there are no absolute facts or contents does not entail that facts or contents cannot show up relative to every conceptual scheme. He writes that "it is rarely, if ever, noticed that metaphysical pluralism is consistent with there being some *virtual absolutes*—facts that do not obtain independently of conceptual schemes but that *do obtain within every scheme*. Pluralism is similarly consistent with virtually absolute propositions, or propositions that are relative to every scheme [italics his]."[21]

15. Ibid., 14.
16. Ibid., 15
17. Ibid., 22.
18. Ibid., 22.
19. Ibid., 53.
20. On the commensurability of perspectives, see Hales, *Relativism*, 40.
21 Lynch, *Truth*, 142.

One of the major issues facing any ontological pluralism is what Lynch calls the "consistency dilemma." This challenge claims that pluralism is entirely unmotivated and, in fact, not even possible. Lynch writes:

> The pluralist alleges that there can be more than one true account of the world. Now consider two such metaphysical perspectives, A and B that meet whatever criteria the pluralist requires for perspectives to be "equally" true. Either these perspectives are consistent with each other or they are not. If not, then by virtue of her statement that A and B are equally true, the pluralist is in danger of being committed to the truth of contradictions. [The] ... pluralist avoids this ... problem by relativization. On her view, facts and content are relative: A can be the case relative to C_1, and -A relative to C_2 without contradiction. But ... this move fails to get the pluralist off the hook. The real problem for pluralism is not the *inconsistency* but the *consistency of schemes*. In other words, given the consistency between A and B that the relativization of fact apparently implies, the pluralist must explain how it is legitimate to talk about *incompatible* but equally true schemes in the first place. Specifically, if A and B are consistent, then either (1) A and B are expressing the same absolute truths in different languages (they are "notational variants") or (2) A and B are simply concerned with different subject matters altogether. But even the most hardheaded absolutist could grant either possibility, for both (1) and (2) are consistent with absolutism [italics his]![22]

This quotation provides the "content" version of the dilemma, but there is a "fact" version as well. It issues in the "many-world" problem in which

> the pluralist is committed either to the existence of many worlds of facts—one world for each conceptual scheme—or to the existence of the one world of facts that all conceptual perspectives are perspectives of. If the former is the case, if there is one world for each conceptual scheme, then not only has the pluralist adopted a bizarre ontology on which worlds are like bubbles insulated from each other by the fragile barriers of concepts, she has apparently committed herself to absolutism. On such a picture, there will be one true story (an absolutely true account) of each individual world. (And the conjunction of those stories will be an absolute account of every world.) On the other hand, if the pluralist holds

---

22. Ibid., 29.

Appendix

that there is only one world that all schemes represent, then presumably there will also be one true account of that world.[23]

The consistency challenge is a serious one and is thought by some to be the death blow to pluralism.

The consistency challenge and a straight-forward reply can be made intuitively clear by an example found in Putnam and repeated by Lynch. Consider Smith and Johnson. Smith and Johnson, let us say, are purveyors of marbles who toy with ontology on the side. Upon looking in a bag containing three marbles, Johnson, who holds to mereological objects,[24] counts exactly seven objects in the bag while Smith, who is no mereologist, counts only but exactly three objects. How is a pluralist to handle this situation? The pluralist, says Lynch, needs to affirm all four of the following propositions:

a. Smith and Johnson are expressing distinct propositions.

b. Smith and Johnson are expressing incompatible propositions.

c. Smith and Johnson are expressing true propositions.

d. Smith and Johnson are not employing completely different concepts of "object" or "exist" or "number"; they are not talking past one another.

The first one is true because "exactly three" implies "not exactly seven" and hence two distinct propositions are being expressed. d.) is true because both ontologists share the same concept of object and existence even though they are extending the concepts in two different, if quite incompatible, directions. c.) is true because "just as it can be true that x is a game in relation to one paradigm example of a game and false relative to another paradigm without this fact causing so much as a whisper of cognitive dissonance, so too is the same move completely acceptable with 'exist' or 'object.'"[25]

That, of course, leaves b.). The consistency dilemma and its reply enters at precisely this point. Quoting Lynch:

> According to the pluralist, [Smith and Johnson] are (or could be) extending their shared minimal concept of an object differently.

---

23. Ibid., 29, 30.

24. The term "mereological" picks out a certain view in metaphysics, including the issue of whether in addition to particular entities (the marbles) there also exist the relationships among the entities (the fact that the red marble is related to the blue, and the blue to the green, and green to the red, and all of them to each other).

25. Ibid., 92.

> Thus the propositions they are expressing are relative to different conceptual schemes and are therefore logically consistent. At the same time, there is a clear and important sense in which the pair of propositions *are* incompatible: *if these propositions were relative to the same scheme, they would be inconsistent.* This fact is necessarily true of that pair of propositions: in every possible world where these propositions are relative to the same scheme, only one is true. And it is in precisely this sense that Johnson and Smith are rightly said to be expressing consistent but incompatible propositions [italics his].[26]

Thus is the consistency dilemma overcome.

The consistency dilemma claims that pluralism is unmotivated and cannot, in fact, even be stated as a distinct view. The absolutist claims that insofar as two propositions are relative to more than one scheme, there must be some absolute framework in which they can both be handled. If they are not relative to more than one scheme but only to their particular schemes, then they "talk past each other" and are not really inconsistent. But as Lynch argues, the propositions involved are not absolute propositions. The truth of the propositions being relative to more than one scheme does not entail that they are independent of all schemes. Minimally a proposition can be relative to more than one scheme, although robustly it cannot. In short, Lynch allows for a minimalist, alethic realism with a pluralist ontology and the consistency dilemma is resolved by appeal to possible world talk. It turns out to be a necessary truth that in every possible world where any two contradictory propositions are relative to the same scheme, only one is true. He can admit this sort of necessary truth precisely because he hasn't lost a realist account of truth. Even though truth is only construed minimally, it is still construed realistically.

III

Before we take up Goodman's irrealism, a brief terminological note. I refer to Goodmans' worlds as "G-worlds" so as to distinguish them as extensionalist actual worlds (with no World "underneath"). This is distinct from the sense of worlds that I proposed above, whose status is rooted in the singular actual World. Having said that, Goodman is not easily characterized in terms of the issues regarding realism. The main reason is that he

---

26. Ibid., 93.

typically rejects the terms of the discussion, sitting askew the issues as they are typically understood. He nevertheless, uses the label "irrealism" that he describes as a radical relativism under rigorous restraints. Here are some general features of his view.

- a. What he calls "world-versions" and "worlds" are not all truth-related. So not all G-worlds (or world-versions) contradict one another
- b. His overall philosophy is committed to nominalism. But his nominalism is not logically connected to his irrealism and hence the construction of various G-worlds.

5. His view, he reports, finds both realism and idealism deplorable as well as acceptable.

Truth is fundamentally connected to the linguistic or what is expressed or expressible by the linguistic. Sentences, utterances, assertions have each been suggested as the bearers of truth, although the proposition is the most popular candidate. The reason for this is not far to seek, for sentences, utterances, and assertions all communicate propositions. When we communicate propositions, we are left with the linguistic.[27] Pictures, gestures, or dances, in contrast, do not communicate propositions and hence are not true. At least, they aren't true in the sense that sentences or assertions are. While the things on this last list (dances, gestures, etc.) can perhaps be said to be true in *some* sense, it is not in the literal sense most of us think of when we say something is true.

Since truth, in the end, seems to be fundamentally connected to the linguistic, it perhaps is odd to understand pluralism in terms other than truths and their linguistic expressions. But this is precisely what Goodman does. He does not limit the conceptual to the linguistic, although he of course admits that lots of our concepts are linguistically expressed. In the opening of their book, *Reconceptions in Philosophy and Other Arts and Sciences*, Goodman and Elgin write, giving a partial account of concepts:

> Nor are concepts and conceptions exclusively linguistic; they may be pictorial, diagrammatic, gestural, kinesthetic or of any other sort. Musical variations are reconceptions that are neither verbal nor replacements for the original version. Moreover, whether the concepts involved are verbal or not, reconception does not always amount to alternation in what is named or described or otherwise

27. I am aware that Goodman, like Quine, likely rejects any notion of proposition that is overly metaphysically thick. I will ignore this aspect of Goodman's larger philosophy.

denoted; it may be in what is exemplified or is expressed or is alluded to indirectly. Thus a change in style or even in vocabulary may sometimes effect a significant reconception.[28]

Concepts are not merely linguistic and although always symbolic in some way, there are many more kinds of symbols and symbol systems than the merely linguistic. Lynch claims that concepts are the constituents of propositions but Goodman denies any exclusivity here. Concepts are sometimes the constituents of things other than propositions. So for Goodman, irrealism is a kind of pluralism where there are many ways things are, some that literally conflict with each other (linguistically based G-worlds) and others that are contrary to each other on grounds other than truth.

Goodman says that there are lots of pairs of conflicting (that is, contradictory) claims that are true descriptions of the way things are. Take the following: "the sun is moving" and "the sun is not moving." How can they be both true, since they seem, straightforwardly, to contradict one another? The problem arises only if we assume there is some one thing having both properties, "moving" and "not moving" said of it, and that what is said of the object is said in the same way, referring to the same time, etc. Truth is truth, so if some thing A is moving and A is also not moving (and we mean the same thing by "moving" in each statement, "A" in each statement, etc.), we get a contradiction. To avoid this contradiction, Goodman concludes that there is no fact of the matter independent of frames of reference. Both "the sun is moving" and "the sun is not moving" are true, and if they are, they must be true in different G-worlds, and hence of different things, on pain of contradiction.

The relativization of claims to frames of reference doesn't resurrect a singular "World," that is, a singular fact of the matter about the sun. Frames of reference belong to systems of description and not to the described entities. One simply cannot say how things are independent of one frame of reference or another.[29] Frames of reference are part of the world-version, the thought, the ideas, the structure for how we organize a G-world. They aren't part of the G-world itself. We bring a frame of reference to the world and behold, the G-world correlated to it is configured a certain way. Relativizing the motion of the sun to frames of reference won't give us a way out of problem of conflicting truths. The ontology (what actually is) is distinct from what determines the ontology (the frame of reference imbed-

28. Goodman and Elgin, *Reconceptions*, vii.
29. Goodman, *Ways*, 2, 3.

ded in a descriptive system). The heliocentric frame of reference and the geocentric frame of reference are part of a system. In this case the system is linguistic and fairly literally so (as opposed to metaphorically so). Both linguistic frames of reference are equally legitimate ways of constructing G-worlds, for we can choose which one to use for one purpose or another. If the linguistic constructions are, so to speak, actually in "the World" then real conflicts ensue. To avoid such conflicts, we must understand the (various) G-worlds to be made up out of various ways of description. Statements within those G-worlds are true (supposing the world actually is the way the description says it is) but to avoid actual contradictions, the G-worlds themselves must be kept separate ontologically from one another. Furthermore, since no one would deny both the geocentric and the heliocentric frames of reference, and because they are both perfectly meaningful, useful, and true, there must be some way of avoiding contradictions with "the World." The only way is to break "the World" asunder and announce the plurality of G-worlds. So, if one tries to make the two statements true of one and the same "World," one ends up with a contradiction. There is no one, singular way "the World" is, but multiple actual G-worlds.

Some world-versions are not linguistic at all, and hence some G-worlds are not linguistically describable. Besides examples such as the motion of the sun, which can, he admits, be transformed into one another, there are the various versions of the world found in various sciences, in the works of various painters and writers, and in our perception. There are not easy or straightforward ways of transforming physics, biology, and psychology into one another. And there is no way at all of transforming any of the scientific versions into Van Gogh's vision, or Van Gogh's into Van Inwagen's.[30] Goodman's overarching point is that there are various symbol systems, some linguistic, some not. These systems can generate not only apparent contradictions (for linguistic systems) but other ways of being disparate as well (for artistic systems or perceptual systems). One can avoid neither the contradictions nor the disparatenesses by discussing frames of reference.

Goodman moves back and forth between world (what I've called "G-world") talk and world-version talk. Sometimes he seems more interested in world-versions than G-worlds: "Our universe, so to speak, consists of these *ways* rather than of a world or of worlds."[31] Other times he seems

30. Ibid., 3.
31. Ibid., 3.

interested in G-worlds rather than their versions, as when he claims that the G-worlds he is interested in are actual and not merely possible worlds. In addition, he talks about "right" (or in other places, "true") versions.[32] Goodman never tells us which is more important, G-worlds or world-versions, nor is he apparently interested in doing so. It seems, in the end, a matter of preference or usefulness.

Systems of description are thus ways of conceptualizing things, whether in scientific or empirical theorizing or just everyday descriptive talk. Yet there are other symbol systems too, systems involving something other than or beyond statements and linguistically based concepts. Some symbol systems involve artistic expression, and these do not involve truth and falsity but other kinds of rightness of rendering such as metaphorical truth, appropriateness of purpose, fittingness to a canvass, etc., or even seeing, which involves perceptual rightness.

As I noted earlier, Goodman understands his view as sitting askew all the traditional categories such as realism and idealism. Goodman describes the idealist as wanting a "singular World." Here perhaps we should think of idealism as a Hegalian- or perhaps Kantian-inspired position. Goodman, however, thinks we have many G-worlds. A noetic irrealist can be either a pluralist or a monist. Apparently Goodman takes his overall irrealistic view to be consistent with either interpretation even though in the end he settles on pluralism. But within a given G-world we can be idealist in the sense he refers to, and will not want, within that G-world, to countenance multiple worlds. But he also says his pluralism is consistent with realism. While his overarching position can't allow him to say what the strict realist wants to say in some final sense ("the World" is independent completely of human noetic contributions—that would be contradictory to irrealism) he can allow again that within a given G-world, that that G-world works on apparent noetic and alethic realist principles. So while a strong noetic realism understood as being "the way things are" would threaten Goodman's irrealism, he seems to set his irrealism above or beyond the fray. Realism and idealism are not, in the end, the issue for Goodman. They are only various ways of talking about things, and not only that, but both ways of talking are merely conventional. Irrealism is a position that simply sits askew the traditional ways of talking about these matters. His view, apparently, is that his irrealism is meta-theoretic rather than working on the level of theory itself.

32. Ibid., 3, 4.

Appendix

Critics suggest that Goodman's nominalism is incompatible with irrealism, for irrealism should be open to Platonism as well. For the irrealist everything, including the individual and classes should be artifacts.[33] On the surface, at least, Goodman easily handles this challenge. If he thinks, as he does, that his irrealism is consistent with various kinds of realism and idealism, it is not a reach to see that it is consistent with nominalism, Platonism, and other possible theories. However, I think Goodman is wrong and that nominalism is incompatible with irrealism. To say why, however, we need a clear picture of Goodman's nominalism, which can be summarized in this way: there are no properties, but predicates bear a one-many relationship to the things they denote. Thus, in one clear sense things are white because they are called white. The application of a one-place predicate to many things requires no properties, but predicates classify (that is, make) or order individuals rather than naming properties or denoting classes or sequences.[34] Classes and properties are not necessary to account for predication. Unlike Quine's nominalism, where the overall classification of things is limited to the physical, Goodman says that to circumscribe the way things are ahead of time is not a complete nominalism. Goodman allows only individuals but puts no limits on what can be taken as an individual. His nominalism, in other words, "bars the composition of different entities out of the same elements."[35] So one will never be able to have more than $2^n - 1$ entities, when the initial number of atomic individuals is n. Whatever one wants to call these compositions—wholes, sums, or even classes—does not matter, so long as none of them contain exactly the same atomic individuals. This, says Goodman, is a nominalism with only individuals.

How does this nominalism fit with irrealism? He says: "Irrealism and nominalism are independent but entirely compatible. Indeed, nominalism neither conflicts with nor implies nor is implied by my other philosophical views."[36] Nominalism commits him to individuals alone but not to what counts as an individual. As such, Goodman's irrealism can be taken in a number of directions each of which is purely conventional: a restricted Platonism, idealism, and even a kind of realism (at least by his own lights). Clearly, nominalism belongs on this list, for we can say the same thing of it,

33. Goodman, *Of Mind*, 29.
34. Ibid., 49.
35. Ibid., 52.
36. Ibid., 30.

viz. Goodman's choice of nominalism is purely conventional. So Goodman's position is not what we might think of as a noetic irrealism merely in contrast with noetic realism. He seems to think that irrealism sits askew these two. Nevertheless, I think most of us are left with the nagging suspicion that insofar as noetic realism is concerned with "the World" being a singular way independent of human noetic contributions, irrealism cannot truly be consistent with noetic realism.

Goodman claims that there are many actual (G-)worlds. He writes: "Why then . . . stress the multiplicity of worlds? In what important and often neglected sense are there many worlds? Let it be clear that the question here is not of the possible worlds that many of my contemporaries, especially those near Disneyland, are busy making and manipulating. We are not speaking in terms of multiple possible alternatives to a single actual world but of multiple actual worlds. How to interpret such terms as 'real,' 'unreal,' 'fictive,' and 'possible' is a subsequent question."[37] There are many actual G-worlds and we can move back and forth between them as easily, sometimes, as simply changing our purposes. An actual world just is a (right) world-version and a right world-version just is an actual world. Which language we prefer is really a difference in emphasis. Goodman's commitment to the actuality of his worlds is simply his commitment to extensionalism. He is ardently opposed to intensionalism and hence to any talk of possible worlds.

One issue central in understanding any irrealism is to grasp how the world-versions or conceptual schemes are related to the worlds—in Goodman's case, G-worlds. Typically, one looks to truth to understand this relation and thus one way to put the issue is to ask how a statement in a world-version is made true by a world. But this belies a significant set of assumptions about world-versions. Goodman will say that not all G-worlds can be thought of in terms of truth and falsity. So we need to cast the net more broadly for Goodman, at least, and ask not merely about truth but rightness.

The statement "a mother bears her child" is ambiguous between "a mother carries her child in her arms" and "a mother gives birth to her child." Goodman's use of the word "truth" is ambiguous in a parallel way. On the one hand, to say that some statement or other is true is to say "'p' is true if and only if p." Thus, a statement bears truth, as if the statement carried its truth in its arms. On the other hand, when Goodman speaks of a

---

37. Goodman, *Ways*, 2.

true world-version he speaks of when a G-world is made, and thus a reality created. This ambiguity can lead to some significant errors in interpreting Goodman, for when he speaks of a true world-version it is natural to think he speaks only of world-versions containing or made of true statements. But for Goodman, while some true world-versions contain true statements, not all do. Only linguistically based true world-versions contain true statements. Hence, not all true versions are simply collections of true statements.

Thus, it is best to reserve the phrase "right world-version" for "true world-version" or to attach the adjective "generative" to "true world-version." So, a right world-version, understood as one that makes a G-world, is a generatively true world-version. Alternatively, we can say that a right world-version has generative truth. However, it is appropriate to claim that along with a rightly rendered descriptive G-world, various statements are made, and thus truths come into being with the G-world made. Here, however, truth (of statements) is secondary (what is made is a G-world and the descriptions are true because of that G-world). Thus, we can allow for a noetic irrealism (a G-world is made via noetic contributions) with an alethic realism (what makes a description true is the G-world as made).

If we are to make sense of the relation between descriptive world-versions and G-worlds, we must stop thinking about truth in traditional terms in which we separate the real from what is made true by the real. We can as easily say "that's the reality" as "that's true." What I mean to call attention to is that in thinking of truth, we must note both sides of the formula—"'p' is true if and only if p." Let me hasten to add that I do not deny or question alethic realism or the basic formula claiming that "p" is true if and only if p. But as Goodman puts it, "saying that there is a star up there and saying that the statement 'There is a star up there' is true amount, trivially, to much the same thing, even though the one seems to talk about a star and the other to talk about a statement."

In order to clarify some issues surrounding truth, I shift our attention now to another kind of rightness. Some concepts are pictorial, gestural, or emotional. We think in concepts, but not all thinking is linguistic or even linguistically describable, even if all concepts are symbolic. When a painter paints a red triangle on a white background it is tempting to say that she is referring to something independent of the painting, namely a red triangle, abstract triangularity, thoughts in the mind of the painter, or something else. Of course, she may very well be referring to or denoting something outside the painting. But she may not be. Not all art imitates or represents. So what is it doing? A painting need not refer, imitate, or represent anything outside the painting at all. Sometimes, indeed, the painting may simply *exemplify* something, as when a paint chip exemplifies the color we want to paint my wife's office. Sometimes a painting can exemplify itself.

The point I want to call attention to is that linguistic symbol systems, although they function in terms of truth and falsity, function in ways parallel to nonlinguistic symbol systems. Sometimes the G-world and the world-version can be separated (as in when a painting is a painting of something else and thus can be said to denote) and sometimes they cannot (as when the painting exemplifies itself). What is often not noted is just how close thing and symbol are in the relationship of true statement to G-world in linguistic symbol systems, even when the thing and symbol are not identical.

Truth is important. Our being aware of, or knowing, the truth enables us to get around in the world(s) in which we live. Too often, however, we separate truth from world in such a way that truths (the symbols) are more valued than what the reality actually is (a world). As I've already noted, we can as easily say "that's the reality" as we can say "that's true." As Alston says, facts and truths, although not exactly the same, come in a tightly bound package.[38] I submit that our desire for truth is a desire for getting things right, and therefore in some sense, truth just is a getting things right. When we get things right, we arrive at the truth. Notice the active, even constructive, nature of both the "getting" and the "arriving" language. I think these are important ways we talk.

We can say that snow is white and we can also say that it is true that, "snow is white." Insofar as we separate these two, we typically say that truth is a property attaching to a truth-value bearer. We might say that we emphasize this within a world-version or at least within a linguistic world-version. Looked at from the other side, however, what is important is not just that the truth-value bearer presents the world well, but that the world itself is present to us. We want reality to be within our access. We can accomplish this philosophically by proposing that we make reality with our noetic feats and hence we have worlds. That reality seems to be within our access is an epistemological issue rather than an ontological one. However, the stand one takes on the ontological issue influences one's stand on the epistemological. Strictly in terms of the issue of truth, however, what is important is giving an account of truth such that saying that p and saying

---

38. Alston, *A Realist Conception*, 239.

the statement "p" is true amount to much the same thing. I believe that the world-version (to which we attribute all kinds of rightness, including truth) and what reality is are very close to one another. Indeed, we can say the two are identical so that whether we say that the world-version is right (generatively true) or that the world is such and such way is, as near as makes no matter, the same. If we can give such an account of truth and rightness, then we will have grasped the importance of truth (and other rightnesses), viz., we've gotten things right.

In some sense, it is a common intuition that truth is trivial. What could be more obvious than the claim that "Snow is white" is true if and only if snow is white? But the statement is opaque too, for we all know the difficulties in formulating a rigorous theory of what truth is, let alone providing the appropriate tests for it. How are we to explain the apparent oddity of the obviously right common intuition of the basic formula and yet the challenges of developing a deep theory? How do we understand the connection between the G-worlds and world-versions? Isn't Goodman just stuck on the world-version side, building one mental sand castle out of another? Put another way, and more pressing for my concerns here, we should ask Goodman exactly how truth is supposed not to collapse into the epistemic creativity of the human mind. How do we get the objectivity that Goodman wants to have?

Part of the answer lies in Goodman's telling us what truth is not. The other part lies in what Goodman's believes is necessary beyond truth. According to Goodman, a world-version is generatively true (whether descriptive, depictive, notational, or what have you) just in case it makes a G-world. True statements are true not because of other statements but because the G-world is the way it is. But there is something further to ask of noetic irrealism, viz., how do statements carry truth? True statements are not true because they "cohere" or are "acceptable" or "epistemically warranted." For Goodman, "p" is true if and only if p. A G-world is the way it is because of a rightly rendered world-version (a generatively true version), and hence what statements are true in that world are true because certain things exist in that G-world. It is in virtue of the G-world, then, that the statements are true, even though the G-world is the way it is because of the version. Noetic irrealism about reality does not preclude alethic realism. In allowing for alethic realism, however, one is not, or need not, affirm anything like a full-fledged correspondence theory of truth. In regard to a minimal account of truth, Goodman says that "saying that there is a star up there and saying that the statement 'There is a star up there' is true amount, trivially, to much the same thing, even though the one seems to talk about a star and the other to talk about a statement." But Goodman also says that the formula "'Snow is white' is true if and only if snow is white" does not commit us to a correspondence theory of truth. Rather it leaves us free to adopt any theory that gives "'Snow is white' is true" and "snow is white" the same truth value.[39]

Although Goodman proposes "ultimate acceptability" as a criterion of truth, he explicitly is not proposing a definition of truth by introducing acceptability as a criterion of it. One supposes the same would be the case with coherence or correspondence (within a world). They are criteria, perhaps, but not definitions of truth. The closest Goodman comes to defining truth is captured, one supposes, with his claim that the formula "'Snow is white' is true if and only if snow is white" commits us only to a theory wherein "'Snow is white' is true" and "snow is white" both have the same truth value. Any theory of truth must be compatible with this minimal formula, so one supposes that the formula isn't about the criteria for truth *per se* but what makes a truth-value bearer true. As we have seen, to be more accurate about the formula we must relativize it to worlds.

---

39. Goodman, *Of Mind*, 48, 49.

Bibliography

Abraham, William. "Turning Theological Water into Wine." *The Journal of Analytic Theology* 1 (2013) 1–16.
Alston, William P. *Perceiving God: The Epistemology of Religious Experience*. Ithaca, NY: Cornell University Press, 1991.
———. "Realism and the Christian Faith." *International Journal for Philosophy of Religion* 31 (1995) 37–60.
———. *A Realist Conception of Truth*. Ithaca, NY: Cornell University Press, 1996.
———. "Referring to God." *International Journal for Philosophy of Religion* 24 (1988) 113–28.
———. *A Sensible Metaphysical Realism*. Milwaukee: Marquette University Press, 2001.
Athanasius. *On the Incarnation*. "Section 54." Online: http://www.ccel.org/ccel/schaff/npnf204.vii.ii.liv.html.
Collins, C. John. *Genesis 1–4: A Linguistic, Literary, and Theological Commentary*. Phillipsburg, NJ: Presbyterian & Reformed, 2006.
Craig, William Lane. "No Other Name: A Middle Knowledge Perspective on the Exclusivity of Salvation through Christ." *Faith and Philosophy* 6 (1989) 172–88.
Crampton, W. Gary. "Christian Exclusivism." *The Trinity Review*. Online: http://www.trinityfoundation.org.
Danto, Arthur. *The Transfiguration of the Commonplace*. Boston: Harvard University Press, 1983.
Date, Christopher, Gregory Stump, and Joshua Anderson, eds. *Rethinking Hell: Readings in Evangelical Conditionalism*. Eugene, OR: Cascade, 2014.
Date, Christopher M., and Ron Highfield, eds. *A Consuming Passion: Essays on Hell and Immortality in Honor of Edward Fudge*. Eugene, OR: Pickwick, 2015.
Dictionary.com http://dictionary.reference.com/browse/image?s=t
DeRose, Keith. "Contextualism and Knowledge Attribution." *Philosophy and Phenomenological Research* 52 (1992) 913–24.
Edwards, Jonathan. "The End of the Wicked Contemplated by the Righteous." Online: http://www.biblebb.com/files/edwards/contemplated.htm.
Goodman, Nelson. *Languages of Art: An Approach to a Theory of Symbols*. Indianapolis: Bobbs-Merrill, 1976.

Bibliography

———. *Of Mind and Other Matters*. Boston: Harvard University Press, 1984.
———. *Ways of Worldmaking*. Indianapolis: Hackett, 1978.
Goodman, Nelson, and Catherine Z. Elgin. *Reconceptions in Philosophy and Other Arts and Sciences*. Indianapolis: Hackett, 1988.
Hales, Steven D. *Relativism and the Foundations of Philosophy*. Boston: MIT Press, 2005.
Hick, John. *An Interpretation of Religion*. 2nd ed. New Haven: Yale University Press, 2005.
Irenaeus. *Against Heresies*. "Book 5, Preface." Online: http://www.ccel.org/ccel/schaff/anf01.ix.vii.i.html.
Kenyon, Stephen, and Mark S. McLeod-Harrison. "Love, Wisdom and Christian Philosophy." In "The Christ-Shaped Philosophy Project." Online: http://www.epsociety.org/library/articles.asp?pid=274.
———. "The Veneration of Truth: How Analytic Theorizing Can Make Us Wise." Forthcoming at *Didaskalia*.
Lynch, Michael. *Truth in Context*. Boston: MIT Press, 2001.
Madueme, Hans. "Adam and Eve: An Evangelical Impasse?—A Review Essay." *Christian Scholar's Review* XLV.2 (2016) 165.
McGrath, Matthew. "Contextualism, Pragmatic Encroachment, and the Knowledge Norm of Assertion." In *Epistemology: A Contemporary Introduction*, edited by Alvin Goldman and Matthew McGrath, 107–30. Oxford: Oxford University Press, 2015.
McLeod-Harrison, Mark S. "God and (Nearly) Global Relativistic Pluralism." *Polish Journal of Philosophy*, 3 (2009) 33–50.
———. "The Many Ways God Is." *Forum Philosophicum*, 14 (2009) 259–76.
———. *Make/Believing the World(s): Toward a Christian Ontological Pluralism*. Montreal: McGill-Queens University Press, 2009.
———. *Repairing Eden: Mysticism, Humility and the Existential Problem of Religious Diversity*. Montreal: McGill-Queens University Press, 2005.
Moser, Paul. *Jesus and Philosophy: New Essays*. Cambridge: Cambridge University Press, 2008.
Moser, Paul, and Michael McFall. "Introduction." In *The Wisdom of the Christian Faith*, edited by Paul Moser and Michael McFall, 1–18. Cambridge: Cambridge University Press, 2012.
Plantinga, Alvin. "A Defense of Religious Exclusivism." In *Philosophy of Religion*, 7th ed., edited by Louis P. Pojman and Michael Rea, 645–59. Belmont, CA: Wadsworth, 1998.
Quinn, Philip L., and Kevin Meeker. *The Philosophical Challenge of Religious Diversity*. Oxford: Oxford University Press, 1999.
Rea, Michael. "Introduction." In *Analytic Theology New Essays in the Philosophy of Theology*, edited by Oliver D. Crisp and Michael C. Rea, 1–30. Oxford: Oxford University Press, 2009.
Schaff, Phillip. "Section 2. The Chalcedonian Statement." In *The New Schaff-Herzog Encyclopedia of Religious Knowledge*, Vol. III. Chamier–Draendorf. Online: http://www.ccel.org/s/schaff/encyc/encyc03/htm/ii.3.4.2.htm.
Southern Baptist Convention. "Basic Beliefs." Website: http://sbc.net.
Walls, Jerry. *Hell: The Logic of Damnation*. Notre Dame, IN: University of Notre Dame Press, 1992.
Ware, Kalistos. "God and Man." Online: http://www.orthodox-christianity.com/2011/03/man-the-fall-free-will-and-grace.

Index

Abraham, William, xv, xvi, 149
absolutist, 38, 131, 135, 137
access, general revelation (GRA), 64–74, 76, 78
access, special revelation (SRA), 64–74, 76
Advaita Vedanta Hinduism, 14, 17, 18
Alston, William P., 2, 16, 17, 56, 61, 91, 91, 93, 97, 103, 133, 145, 149
analytic theology, xv-xviii, 150
antirealism, 17, 18, 46, 88, 93
antirealist, 14, 16, 17, 85, 93,
Athanasius, 107, 108, 108, 123, 123, 124, 149
Augustine of Hippo, 107

Basil of Caesarea, xv, 107

Chalcedon confession, 115
Christian salvific pluralism, 1
Clayton, Philip, 99
Clement of Alexandria, 107
Collins, C. John, 111, 149
concept, xv, xvi, 27, 36, 37, 82–84, 91, 95, 99–101, 112, 128–36, 138, 139, 141, 144
concept, minimal, 83, 84, 131, 133, 136
concepts, crystalline, 36
concepts, fluid, 36, 130

conceptual scheme, 37–39, 43, 82, 83, 86, 87, 90–97, 99–103, 105, 119, 128–30, 132–35, 137, 143
consistency dilemma, vii, 135–37
contextualism, 52, 53, 149, 150
Craig, William Lane, x, 49, 49, 59–65, 67–72, 75–78, 149
Crampton, W. Gary, 8, 10, 149

Dante, 75
Danto, Arthur, 24, 149
Date, Christopher, 75, 149
deflationary theory, 17, 132
DeRose, Keith, 53, 53, 149
Descartes, 27
Dictionary, 29

Earl, Harley, 32
Edwards, Jonathan, 77, 78, 149
Elgin, Catherine Z., 138, 139, 150,
epistemic defeaters, 56
exclusivism, access, ix,x, 2, 7, 58, 59
exclusivism, Christian salvific (CSE), xi, xiii, 1–3, 6, 9–14, 18, 45–51, 54–57, 60, 61, 81, 84, 96, 101
exclusivism, ontological, ix, 60
existential, vii, xv-xvii, xix, 11, 45–48, 51, 54–57, 81, 92, 99, 101, 102, 104, 150
expansivism, x, 19, 81, 99, 102
extra epistemological, 51, 52, 56

Index

faith, xi-xv, xvii, 2–15, 17, 38, 46, 48, 50, 55–58, 61–63, 65, 66, 71–74, 76, 79, 83, 91, 92, 95, 97, 98, 100, 101, 106, 107, 149, 150

Goodman, Nelson, 38, 38, 39, 84, 125, 129, 129, 137–44, 146, 147, 147, 149, 150
Graham, Billy, 13
Gregory of Nazianzus, 107

Hales, Steven D., 125, 126–28, 134, 150
Hick, John, 16, 17, 18, 150
hiddenness-of-God, 50
Highfield, Ron, 149
human nature, 22, 71, 119

image, dichotomous, 24, 25, 27, 28, 30, 42, 112, 114, 115, 118–20
image, of God, vii, xix, xxii, 1, 20–24, 31–36, 40–43, 44, 81, 100, 103, 104–16, 118–20, 122–24
image, presentational, 31, 32, 41, 42, 113, 118, 120–24
images, typifying, 29–31, 37, 120, 121
inclusivism, ix, x, xii, 58–61, 67–70, 75, 76, 81, 98, 101,
inclusivism, Christian salvific (CSI), 1, 13, 14, 18, 19, 81
inclusivist, broad-access, 62
inclusivist, narrowly, 63
interior framework, 5
Irenaeus, 107, 107, 108, 123, 124, 150

Kenyon, Stephen, xvi, 150

Luther, Martin, 4, 11, 48,
Lynch, Michael, 82, 83, 93, 125, 128–37, 139, 150

Madueme, Hans, xviii
McFall, Michael, xvi, 150
McGrath, Matthew, 53, 53, 150
McLeod-Harrison, Mark S., x, xvi, 17, 18, 57, 75, 85, 90, 150
Meeker, Kevin, x, 150
metaphysical realist, 2, 45, 47, 85, 86, 92,

Moser, Paul, xvi, xvi, 150

naïve realist, 9
Nicene Creed, 94, 96

ontological monistic, 2

perspectivalism, 90
philosophy, Christian, xv, xvi, 150
philosophy, pastoral, xv-xvii
Plantinga, Alvin, 56, 56, 150
Plato, 23, 24, 32, 35, 142,
pragmatic, 53, 54, 150
properties, essential, 20–22, 24, 34–40, 119–21
properties, thick, 36, 37, 93, 94
properties, thin, 36, 37, 39, 40, 42, 83, 93, 94, 101
properties, Wittgensteinian resemblance, 39

Quine, Willard Van Orman, 138, 142
Quinn, Philip L., x, 150

Rea, Michael, xv, 150
realism, metaphysical, 2, 13, 17, 18, 46, 47, 81, 84, 85, 91, 98, 149
relativism, 83, 88, 90, 125–28, 134, 138, 150
representation, 25–28, 30–34, 38, 39, 113

salvific religious pluralism (SRP), xi, 13, 14, 16–18, 99,
sanctification, xvii, xx, 8, 10, 42, 65, 66, 106, 107
Schaff, Phillip, 107, 108, 115, 149, 150
Smith, Philip, xxii, 73,
Southern Baptist Convention, 10, 10, 61, 61, 62, 150
Strawson, Peter, 82, 129

theistic irrealism, vii, x, 19, 81, 82, 94, 97–100, 102, 103, 125
thin essence, 36, 37, 119

Walls, Jerry, 75, 150
Ware, Kalistos, 111, 112, 150

Index

Wittgenstein, Ludwig, 36, 37, 39, 40, 129, 130

worldview, xvii, 18, 82, 84, 128–30, 133, 134,

www.ingramcontent.com/pod-product-compliance
Lightning Source LLC
Chambersburg PA
CBHW030114170426
43198CB00009B/617